Embroidery & Patchwork
REVISITED

An Illustrated Guide to Hand Stitching
by Janice Vaine

Landauer Publishing, LLC

Embroidery & Patchwork Revisited

An Illustrated Guide to Hand Stitching
by Janice Vaine

Dedication

This book is dedicated to my Mom, Luella Dusek. She taught me from a very young age to love all things needle and thread. She is my encouragement and inspiration.

Copyright © 2014 by Landauer Publishing, LLC

Original projects, text, patterns, and illustrations copyright © 2014 by Janice Vaine. All rights reserved.

This book was designed, produced, and published
by Landauer Publishing, LLC
3100 101st Street, Urbandale, IA 50322
800-557-2144; 515-287-2144; www.landauerpub.com

President/Publisher: Jeramy Lanigan Landauer
Vice President of Sales and Administration: Kitty Jacobson
Editor: Jeri Simon
Art Director: Laurel Albright
Technical Illustrator: Lisa Christensen
Photographer: Sue Voegtlin

Advertising and Marketing Manager: McB McManus
Digital Marketing Manager: E.B. Updegraff

This book is printed on acid-free paper.

Printed in United States: 10 9 8 7 6 5 4 3 2 1

Library of Congress Control Number: 2013951579

ISBN 13: 978-1-935726-51-7

Table of Contents

One never knows when inspiration will strike. Inspiration struck me head on as I ascended an escalator at the 2012 Spring Quilt Market in Kansas City. I was mesmerized by the beauty and uniqueness of an antique quilt—not really a crazy quilt, yet more than a patchwork quilt—distinctly displayed in the Quilts by Mulberry Lane's booth. As the escalator slowly moved upward bringing me closer to this awe-inspiring quilt, my mind was racing with the possibilities it offered. Stepping off the escalator and seeing it close up, I was captivated by the simplicity of the stitches, the distinctive embroidered motifs, the limited thread colors, and the definite order of design.

This beautiful antique quilt now hangs above a bed in our home and has literally become a quilt to dream under. Since acquiring the quilt in 2012, I often wonder about the woman who graced the quilt with her stitches. Who was she? How did she decide which stitches, threads, and colors to use for the patchwork and embroidery? What inspired her to make the oak leaf wreath throughout the center Dresden plate? Were the embroidered motifs original designs or boilerplate designs of the time? Did she feel the monotony of working 200 plus bullion loops or did she count a blessing with each stitch? What inspired her to quilt the quilt versus tying the quilt top and backing together as was the practice of the time? What were her hopes and dreams and thoughts as she stitched the top? How did she come by the fabrics that are in the quilt? Did others help her stitch blocks for the quilt? Was the quilt for a special occasion? How long did she work on this quilt?

As this exquisite quilt was replicated, many happy events occurred. Sons, daughters, and step-daughters were married, first grandbabies were born, new puppies were a welcome addition to families, good medical prognoses were heard, mission trips were shared, friendships grew, and a 60th wedding anniversary celebrated. All of these blessed occasions gave those of us recreating the quilt pause as we dreamed of what the future held for the wee ones welcomed to our families, for the married life of the newlyweds, and for the ebbs and flow of family life. These events caused us to reflect back on the blessings and

trials of life. The hours stitching on a quilt such as this truly makes it A Quilt to Dream Under.

Carolyn and Don Springer lovingly cared for and enjoyed the beauty and grandeur of this inspiring antique quilt in their home. In 2012 they decided it was time to share the quilt with another. I feel blessed the Springers' paths were crossed with mine and that I now have guardianship of this quilt. It is my prayer that through this book many others will have the opportunity to enjoy the artistry of this antique quilt and the honored needlewoman's labor of love.

Don and Carolyn Springer
Quilts by Mulberry Lane

A Quilt to Dream Under

As quilters, we love color, texture, and the creativity a quilt offers.
Crazy quilts lend themselves to all of these things. While I have always
admired these quilts, the idea of making a crazy quilt block foundation,
or an entire quilt, was a challenge for me. I like order and a game plan to
follow when constructing a block and quilt. Crazy quilts just by their
name imply an insane order and freewheeling spirit. There is no set color or
fabric order, no order to piecing or the size of the pieces. In vintage
quilts, fabric was chosen and used based on its shape and whether it fit
together with the other fabric puzzle pieces. And yet, in my orderly world
I am drawn to this beautiful art form and decided to take the challenge.

Supplies

Notions:

Rotary cutter

Rulers: 6½" x 12½" ruler with ¼" markings, 6½" x 24½" ruler, and 18½" square ruler

Double-stick tape

Small wooden pressing tool

Clover Mini Iron™

Small wooden cutting board

Artist tracing paper

Fine-point felt tipped permanent marking pen

Transfer-Eze™

Tricot knit fusible interfacing for wools, silks, velvet, or loosely woven fabrics

Loew-Cornell® transfer paper

Chalk pouncer

Sewline™ Trio Marking Pen

Pigma® Micron® .05 Archival Pen

Silver Gelly Roll™ Pen

Needles for embroidery:

Chenille needles: Size 18-24

Crewel needles: Size 3-8

Straws (Milliners): Size 9-11

Tapestry: Size 18-24

Threads:

50 wt. or 60 wt. cotton thread in neutral colors for machine piecing

6-stranded embroidery floss in colors to complement and accent the patchwork

Perle Cotton 3, 5, and 12 in colors to complement and accent the patchwork

1-ply or 2-ply crewel wool

Fabric for Patchwork Blocks:

Patchwork: Assorted pieces of cotton, linen, silk, wool, and/or velvet

Cotton flannel: 20" square

Backing: 18½" square

Needles and Threads

"Which needle and thread do I use for this stitch?" This is the question most often asked in hand embroidery classes. The simple answer is, use a needle with the shaft or diameter of the needle slightly larger than the thickness of the thread. The eye of the needle should be large enough to allow the thread to pass through easily. The needle will then make a hole in the fabric large enough for the thread to pass through while preventing the thread from fraying and breaking. In this case bigger is not better. If the needle is too big it will leave a hole that cannot be filled with the thread which will cause uneven stitches.

Certain types of needles work best with specific types of embroidery and threads. Refer to the chart on page 9 to determine the correct needle to use. Note the variety of the eye shape and length, the length of the needle shaft, and the point of the needle, sharp or blunt. The size of a needle is designated by a number. The higher the number, the smaller and finer the needle.

NEEDLE	SIZE	THREAD	USE
Chenille— thick shaft, large eye, sharp point	18-24	Thick threads, such as tapestry wool, crewel wool, six strands of stranded cotton, perle cotton 3 and 5, thick silk, and heavy metallic thread. Also for 2mm to 13mm silk ribbon.	Ribbon and wool embroidery
Crewel (Embroidery)— fine shaft, large oval eye, sharp point	9-10	One or two strands of cotton, silk, and rayon	Fine embroidery
	3-8	Three to six strands of stranded cotton, silk or rayon, coton a broder, broder medicis, perle cotton 8 and 12, and fine metallic thread	No. 7 ideal for smocking Excellent general purpose needles
Sharps— medium shaft, small round eye, sharp point	10-12	One or two strands of stranded cotton, silk or rayon	Fine embroidery Bullions
	7-9	Two or three strands of stranded cotton, silk or rayon	
Straw (Milliners)— long, fine shaft, tiny eye, sharp point	9-11	One or two strands of stranded cotton, silk or rayon	Beading Bullions
	5-8	Three or four strands of stranded cotton, silk or rayon	Brazilian embroidery that uses Rayon Viscoe thread
	1-4	Four to six strands of stranded cotton, silk or rayon, perle cotton 8 and 12, coton a broder and metallic threads, and thick twisted threads	Traditionally used for work on bonnets and hats
Tapestry— medium length, thick shaft, long oval eye, rounded blunt tip *Note: The blunt tip separates the fabric rather than splitting the threads of the fabric.*	26-28	Fine braid metallic threads, blending filament, one or two strands of stranded cotton	Decorative hem stitching Fine counted cross stitch
	18-24	Thick threads such as tapestry wool, crewel wool, six strands of stranded cotton, perle cotton 3 and 5, thick silk and heavy metallic thread	Counted thread embroidery such as cross stitch, blackwork, pulled and drawn work Hardanger, wool embroidery, needleweaving, and shadow work

There are many types of threads available for use in hand embroidery, from cottons to silks to wools to metallics, solid colorfast threads to beautiful overdyes, all in varying weights and plys. Each has its own unique characteristic and produces different effects. A needle artist in a thread shop is like a child in a candy store. Play and experiment with stitches in a variety of threads and colors. Let your creativity and imagination paint a canvas of stitches.

THREADS		
Stranded Cotton (embroidery floss)—very versatile thread that typically consists of six fine strands. It can be divided to use one to six strands or blended with different colored threads.	The Gentle Art 0390 Buckeye Scarlet	
Stranded Silk—typically consists of 12 fine strands of thread. Very high sheen. It is used the same way as stranded cotton.	Splendor™ 12 ply silk S1006 Belle Soie 12 ply silk Tulip	
Perle Cotton—a single strand of twisted mercerized cotton. It is excellent for textured effects. Available in 3 (heavy), 5, 8, and 12 (fine).	3—DMC® 321 5—Weeks Dye Works™ 2266 Turkish Red 8—Valdani M43 12—DMC® 814, Wonderfil SP08	
Soft Embroidery Cotton—a matte thread with a soft, muted appearance. Good for interlaced or whipped stitches.	Impressions® by Caron 3041	
Coton a Broder—a single strand of cotton thread available in sizes 12, 16, 20, 25, 30, and 35. Also available in a wide range of colors.	Tentakulum Painter's Thread 111 Frida	
Metallic—real or synthetic fiber available in a wide range of weights and texture. It can be used with other threads to highlight stitches.	Kreinik Metallics 12 Braid 003	
Crewel Wool—fine, 2-ply yarn that can be used singly or in multiple strands.	The Gentle Art 0390-W Buckeye Scarlet	
Persian Wool—available in stranded form that can be used as a single thread or combined.	Paternayan® 940	
Tapestry Wool—single strand that is good for couching.	Laine Colbert 7108	
Knitting Yarns—available in wool, cotton, and synthetic fibers that are good for couching.	Knitted Wit - Gumballs	
Rug Wool—heavyweight wool yarns good for couching.	Lamb's Pride Ruby Red	

The Blocks

The finished blocks used throughout the book are made up of a combination of four different patchwork blocks. This gives the variety and "crazy" look we are trying to achieve with little effort.

The four patchwork blocks are constructed in the same manner. There are five pieces in each block. The pieces are numbered 1 through 5 and sewn together in numerical order beginning with piece 1.

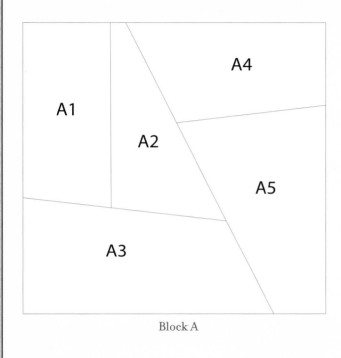

Block A

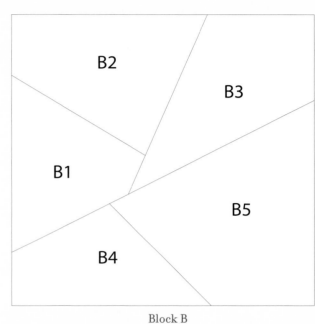

Block B

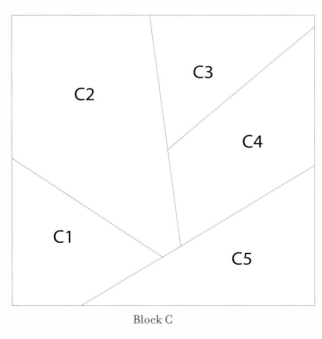

Block C

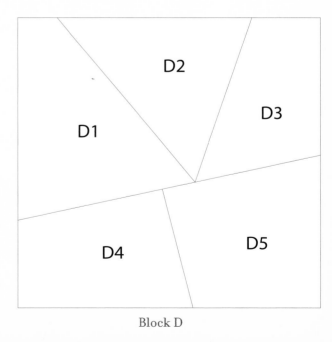

Block D

CUTTING INSTRUCTIONS

1. Using a rotary cutter and ruler, cut out the numbered templates (pages 31-45) for each block. Leave an ⅛" seam allowance around the outside edge. This allows you to clearly see the edge of the template when cutting out the fabric pieces.

   Note: See page 20 for the Curved Piecing Option, as well as tips for using curved templates A3, B3, C5, and D1 on pages 46-47 in the block construction.

   Tips: Place each Block Map and the corresponding block templates in a sheet protector. This will keep you organized as you make each block.

   Back wools, silks, velvets or loosely woven fabrics with a piece of Transfer-Eze™ or tricot knit fusible interfacing. This stabilizes the bias edges for controlled piecing without adding bulk to the fabric.

2. Center a piece of double-stick tape on the wrong side of each template. The double-stick tape will help hold the template in place while cutting out the fabric.

Gather the fabrics you want to use in your blocks. Allow yourself freedom in choosing fabrics and colors. Select colors and fabrics you would not normally try together.

3. Place Template A1 on a piece of fabric, both should be right sides up. Using the rotary cutter and a 6½" x 12½" ruler, cut around the template ADDING A ¼" SEAM ALLOWANCE around the entire outside edge. Adding the seam allowance to the fabric prevents the paper template from being cut or trimmed. The template will remain accurate as you cut additional pieces. Cut out all the templates for Blocks A through D.

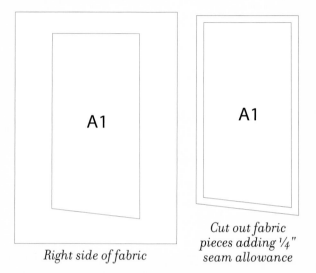

Right side of fabric

Cut out fabric pieces adding ¼" seam allowance

Tips: Place all the fabrics you are using in the block or quilt in a paper bag. Pull out one piece at a time (without looking inside the bag) and cut out a template with the pulled piece of fabric. Continue pulling and cutting until all the templates have fabric attached. When you piece your block, you will be amazed at how unique each block appears.

Cut all your templates and arrange the blocks. If there is a piece of fabric you feel does not fit with all the others, replace it now before your blocks are sewn together.

Take a picture of the block before piecing to see if you like the effect.

Piecing the Patchwork Blocks

General Instructions:

Seam allowances are ¼" unless otherwise noted.

Pressing:

- Press seams open unless otherwise noted.

- When sewing a lightweight and heavyweight fabric together, press the seam toward the lightweight fabric.

- Be careful to press using an iron setting for the fabric being pressed. For instance, do not use a cotton setting to press silk or wool as it may burn the fabric. Consider using a small wooden press for delicate fabrics.

- When pressing a seam with multiple fabric weights, clip the seam to press toward the lighter weight fabric. Press seams open when the fabric weights are similar. For example, press cotton seams open. Press silk seams open. Press a cotton and wool seam to the cotton.

Block Construction:

- This method is forgiving when it comes to piecing. All four blocks are oversized. Once they are constructed, each block will be trimmed square. When the four blocks are pieced together to make one large block, it is also oversized. After the block is embroidered, it is then trimmed to size.

- Using the Block Maps as your guide, lay out the templates with the fabric attached. Remove the templates only when you are ready to sew pieces together. Place them in a sheet protector to stay organized.

Block A

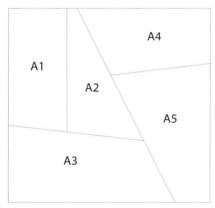

Block Map A

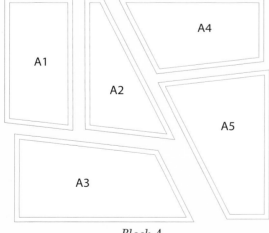

*Block A
templates with fabric*

Referring to the arrows on the diagrams, sew the block pieces right sides together. Press seams after each piece is added.

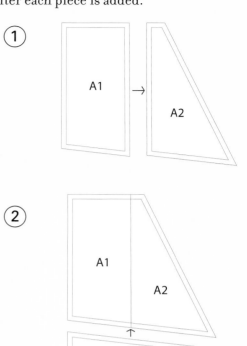

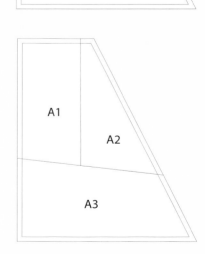

Tip: If a two-pieced section does not have an even edge to join to the third piece, trim the joining edges even. Remember the blocks are oversized and have a little wiggle room when it comes to piecing.

Block A *continued*

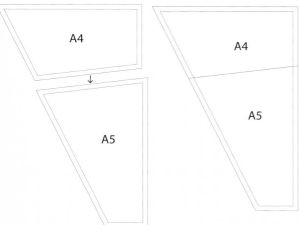

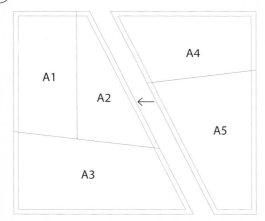

Block B

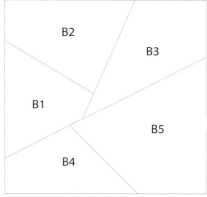

Block Map B

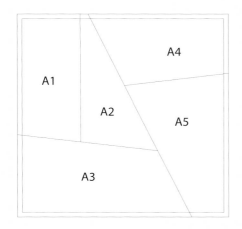

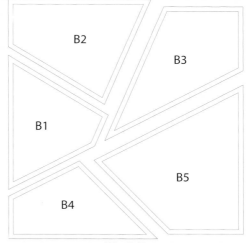

*Block B
templates with fabric*

Block B *continued*

Referring to the arrows on the diagrams, sew the
block pieces right sides together. Press seams
after each piece is added.

 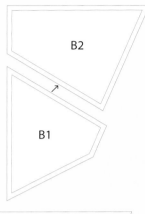

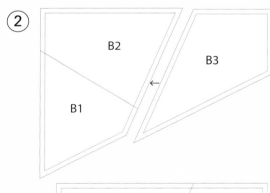

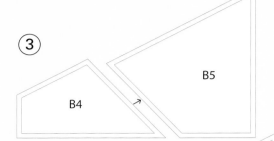

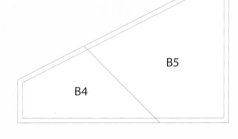

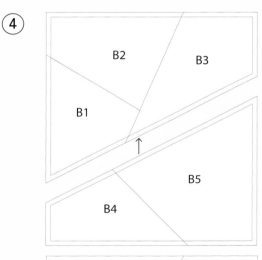

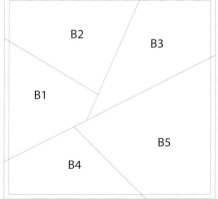

Block C

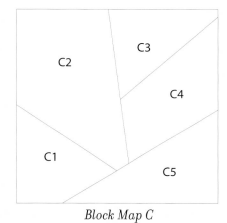

Block Map C

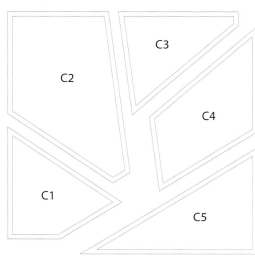

*Block C
templates with fabric*

Referring to the arrows on the diagrams, sew the block pieces right sides together. Press seams after each piece is added.

①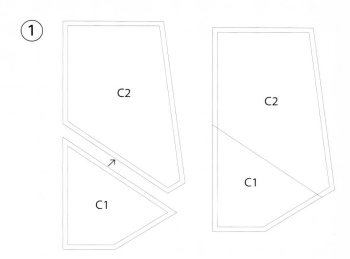

②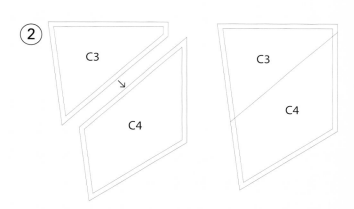

③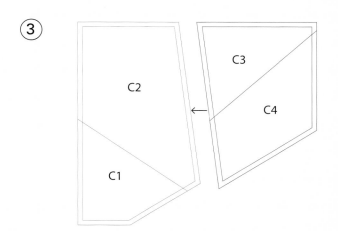

Block C *continued*

④

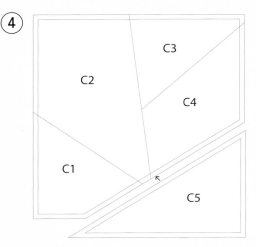

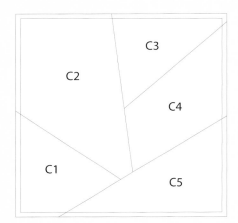

Block D

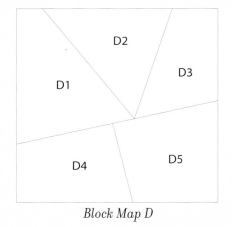

Block Map D

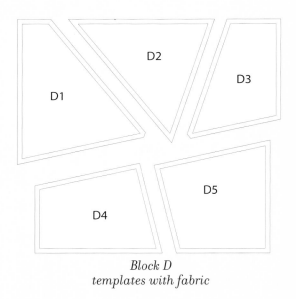

*Block D
templates with fabric*

Block D *continued*

Referring to the arrows on the diagrams, sew the
block pieces right sides together. Press seams
after each piece is added.

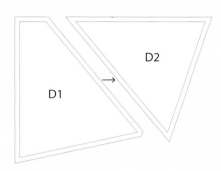
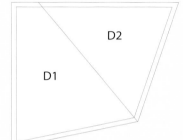

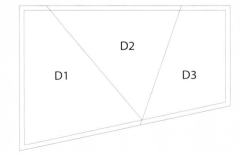
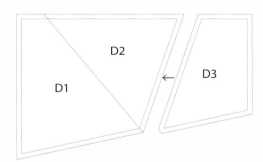

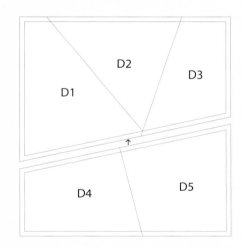
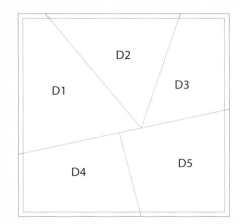

Curved Piecing Option

Referring to the diagrams shown, cut out the numbered A3, B3, C5, and D1 templates on pages 46-47 for each curved block option. The curved edges give the blocks a softer appearance. Here are some tips and tricks for using the optional curved templates:

1. Cut a curved edge using your rotary cutter and ruler. Gently turn the ruler around the curved edge as you cut, maintaining a ¼" seam allowance.

2. Center the curved template on the wrong side of the fabric. There should be a ¼" fabric seam allowance on the curved edge. Gently press the curved seam allowance of the fabric

piece over the edge of the template using a Clover Mini Iron™.

3. Place the curved edge of the fabric on the right side of the adjoining fabric piece and pin. Machine or hand baste along the edge of the curve. This edge will be covered with embroidery stitches.

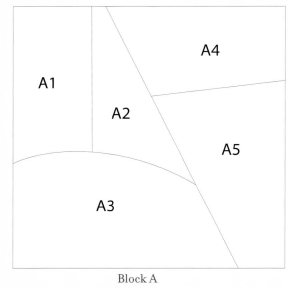
Block A

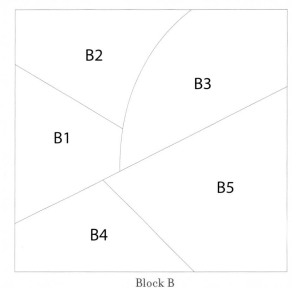
Block B

Block C

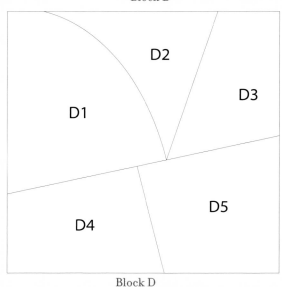
Block D

Making the Sampler Block

1. Square up each of the patchwork blocks (A–D) to 10½" x 10½".

Tip: Use four of the same blocks or any combination of Blocks A through D. When making a larger quilt, this makes all the finished blocks look unique.

2. Rotate the four blocks to achieve a pleasing configuration of colors, fabrics, and shapes. Sew two of the blocks together, as shown. Press. Repeat with remaining two blocks.

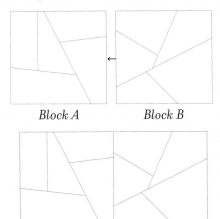

Block A   *Block B*   *Block C*   *Block D*

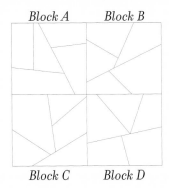

3. Sew the block pairs together as shown to make a sampler block. Press. On the right side of the block, draw an 18½" square. This will be the guideline for the boundaries of your embroidery.
    Note: The block is oversized to accommodate for any shrinkage from the embroidery.

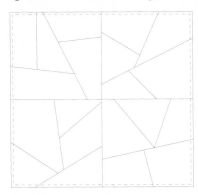

Block A   *Block B*

Block C   *Block D*

4. Place the sampler block on top of the 20" x 20" cotton flannel square. Pin. Machine baste the block horizontally, vertically, and diagonally. Baste around the 18½" square marked on the block.

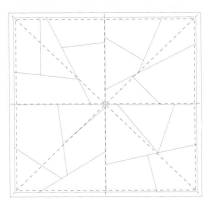

Embroidering the Sampler Block

Your sampler block is now ready to be complemented with touches of embroidery.

Typically each pieced seam on a crazy quilt is covered with embroidery stitches. The vintage method of piecing a crazy quilt block involved turning under the edges of each piece and basting them together. The seams were then permanently held together with the embroidery stitches.

In this case, your sampler block is firmly machine stitched together making the embroidery stitches strictly decorative. The fun and creativity of a crazy quilt comes from choosing the thread, stitches, and designs to cover the pieced blocks. There is no right or wrong stitch or thread selection.

There are 19 basic embroidery stitches on pages 50-73. Choose from a range of these to embellish your sampler block. Stitch combinations are also suggested on pages 130-133. If you are new to embroidery, you may want to practice the stitches on a piece of muslin. If you are an experienced embroiderer, it may be helpful to stitch samples in different threads for a variety of options for your block. Otherwise, just go for it and stitch away on your sampler block.

Much like creating your patchwork blocks with different fabrics and colors, you are free to use various threads, colors, stitches, and stitch combinations. Experiment, have fun and be warned, it will become addictive.

Tip: Gain inspiration from the Stitch Combinations on pages 130-133. Those who stitched the projects and quilts in this book created and inspired these combinations.

Sampler Block

1. Refer to the finished blocks in the "A Quilt to Dream Under" quilt, shown above and on page 94, as a guide to embroider your sampler block or as inspiration for choosing your own stitches.

2. Embroider each seam with a different stitch (pages 50-73) or stitch combination (pages 130-133). Add motifs (pages 134-143). Remove any basting stitches that intersect your embroidery stitches and motifs. Be creative as you choose different threads and colors to embroider.

Tip: Be sure to work the lines of embroidery stitches to the outside edges of the marked and basted 18½" square block. When the block is trimmed to size, the lines of stitches will be secured in the seams of the finished block.

Refer to pages 26-27 for general instructions on marking and embroidering the motifs on your blocks.

Embroidery Techniques

The following information will ensure your embroidery experience is enjoyable and successful.

Pouncing the Thread

Pouncing separates stranded embroidery floss into individual threads. The strands are then placed back together for stitching. The number of strands used depends on the thickness of the desired stitch. The stripping or separating of stranded floss makes your stitches fuller, smoother, and more consistent.

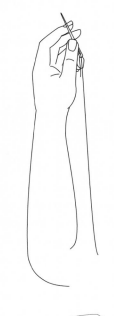

1. Cut a length of thread no longer than 18". A good rule of thumb is a length of thread from the tip of your forefinger to your elbow. This length will alleviate fraying and thread breakage.

2. Hold the cut end of the thread between your forefinger and thumb with 1" of thread above your fingers. Pounce the end of the threads by lightly tapping the cut end with the forefinger of your other hand. If the threads blossom apart, pull out an individual strand from this end. If it does not blossom, try pouncing the other end.

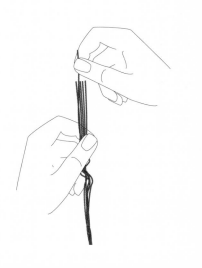

3. Pull a single thread from among the others. The remaining threads will gather below your thumb and forefinger. Lay the individual thread on a flat surface. Repeat until all the threads have been stripped or separated. Lay the desired number of threads back together and all in the same direction.

Needles

Your needles need to be sharp, fine, and good quality. Low quality needles often come with small imperfections that snag fabric and fray thread.

Needles come in a variety of sizes. A number identifies the needle's size. The higher the needle number the smaller or finer the needle shaft. It is important to match the size of the needle with the selected thread. If the needle is too large, it will leave a hole in the fabric too large to be filled by the thread. If the needle is too small, it will stress the thread as it passes through the fabric.

My general rule of thumb for choosing the correct needle is the thread should easily pass through the eye of the needle and the shaft of the needle should be slightly thicker than the diameter of the thread. The doubled thread at the eye of the needle should easily pass through the hole made by the needle without stressing or damaging the thread.

Refer to the needle chart on page 9 when matching needles and threads.

To Hoop or Not to Hoop

An embroidery hoop is used to hold fabric taut while embroidering. It helps keep stitches even and consistent. Some embroiderers find certain stitches easier to work without a hoop. Several questions arise when it comes to hooping patchwork blocks. What do you do with delicate fabrics like silks and velvets that could be marred by a hoop? Do you hoop over the embroidered seams and motifs as you continue to work in another area of the block or quilt top?

I prefer hooping my embroidery as I feel my stitches are more consistent. However, during this project I found myself stitching without a hoop in many areas of the quilt projects. The blocks were stabilized with muslin or flannel to maintain the quality of the hand embroidery stitches.

Multiple projects in the book back the patchwork blocks with flannel giving the fabric a stability to stitch on without a hoop. The 'fuzzy' side of the flannel adheres well to the back of the pieced block. For the smaller fan blocks muslin was used on the back. Since the fan blocks had minimal stitching, the muslin was the perfect weight.

My sewing basket contains 5", 7", 10", and 14" embroidery hoops. I stitch with the size hoop that closely fits the area of my embroidery. I often start with a smaller hoop and work up in size.

When hooping patchwork blocks for embroidery, it is important to take steps to protect the needlework when the hoop does not fit the full area to be embroidered.

- Wrap the inner hoop with strips of cotton muslin or thin cotton batting. Add a few stitches to the end of the wraps to hold the strips in place. This helps pad and protect the stitches.

- Before hooping, place tissue paper over the area to be hooped. Place the work in the hoop and tear the tissue paper away from the working area. This will help protect the stitches that have already been worked and keep the rest of the hooped area from hand oils that may attract dirt.

- Always release the hoop when you are not stitching. Leaving your work in the hoop can cause permanent marks on your fabric.

Note: I recently had an opportunity to try an innovative hand embroidery and quilting hooping system developed by Sharon Schamber of Schamber Quilts, Sharon Schamber's Hoop-Dee-Doo™. It uses an embroidery hoop, but you are not placing the fabric between the rings of the hoop. The hoop supports the embroidery without causing any stress on previous stitches. It also eliminates the possible marring of delicate silks, velvets, and wools when they are placed in a hoop. The system will work with any size or brand embroidery hoop, quilting hoop, or machine embroidery hoop. It is the perfect solution when it comes to making the decision, to hoop or not to hoop. See Resources on page 144 for product information.

Hooping Your Work

1. Place the inner and outer rings of the hoop together. Tighten the screw so the outer ring fits snugly over the inner ring.

2. Loosen the screw just enough to pop the rings apart.

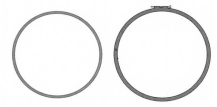

3. Place the inner ring on a flat surface. Place the fabric on top of the inner ring with the stitching area centered over the ring.

4. Fit the outer ring over the fabric and onto the inner ring. Keep both rings parallel when sandwiching the fabric between them. You will hear a "pop" as the two rings are joined. The fabric should be taut and smooth. Do not pull the fabric to smooth it as this may distort the weave and grain of the fabric, causing distorted designs. For example, a stitched circle would become an oval when released from the hoop if the fabric is pulled to tighten it. If the fabric is not taut and smooth, remove the outer ring, tighten the screw, and repeat steps 3-4.

Beginning and Ending Stitching—
The Waste Knot

1. Thread the needle and knot the end of the thread. Insert the needle and thread into the fabric from front to back, 4"-6" from the beginning of the stitching line. The waste knot, or thread knot, is resting on the top of the fabric. This knot will be removed later, Begin working your line of embroidery stitches.

Waste knot is on the right side of the fabric

2. When you finish a line of embroidery stitches, take the needle and thread to the wrong side of the fabric. Make a Buttonhole Stitch (page 51) over the last stitch. Weave the needle and thread through several of the completed stitches. Cut the thread.

Wrong side   *Wrong side*

3. Cut the waste knot on the front of the fabric. Rethread the needle on the wrong side. Knot and weave the waste knot thread in the same manner as the embroidery thread in step 2.

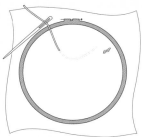 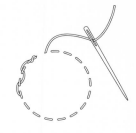

Right side
Cut and remove waste knot

Wrong side
Knot and weave
the waste knot thread

Marking Designs On The Fabric

Choose a design (pages 134-143) to add your touch of needle artistry to the block. In order to stitch a design, it must be transferred onto the right side of the fabric. Experiment with the following techniques to mark designs on the fabric.

Tip: Before marking and stitching your chosen design, remove any basting stitches that fall within the design area on your block.

Artist Tracing Paper

There are several benefits to using this paper. It works on most fabrics, it is easy to see where to center your design, and no marks are left on the fabric. This method works well with textured and heavier fabrics, such as wool and velvet. The traced lines are finer and smoother on the tracing paper as opposed to lines traced directly onto heavier fabric or over seams.

1. Trace your chosen design onto the artist tracing paper using an extra fine felt tipped marking pen. Allow the ink to dry. Trim around the design leaving ½" of tracing paper.

2. Center the design on the block and pin in place. Baste the tracing paper to the fabric.

3. Embroider the design working through the tracing paper and fabric. The designs may be stitched with the Backstitch (page 50), Chain Stitch (page 56), or Stem Stitch (page 70).

4. When your embroidery is finished, gently tear away the tracing paper. Use your needle to score the tracing paper close to the stitches and fine tweezers to remove the paper. Be careful not to pull too hard and distort your stitches. Patience is key in removing the tracing paper.

Tip: Trace multiple designs onto the artist tracing paper. Cut out each individual motif leaving ½" of tracing paper around the outside of the design. Arrange motifs on the block to achieve your desired effect. Take a picture to remember the placement of each motif. Baste each in place when ready to stitch. This will speed your design decisions and stitching time.

Prick & Pounce

This is a very reliable method of transferring a design to any fabric, from silks to cottons to linens and wools. Although it is a bit labor intensive, it is accurate. Once the pattern is prepared, it can be used again and again.

1. Trace or print the pattern on a piece of vellum or artist tracing paper.

2. Using a #10 embroidery needle, prick the pattern following all the lines. The pricked holes should be approximately ¹⁄16" apart. Make sure you place a pricked hole at the beginning and end of each line.

Tip: Place the pattern on a pillow to prick the holes.

3. Center the design on the block. Place the rough side of the pricked design down on the fabric. Pin the corners of the design or weigh them down to hold the pattern in place.

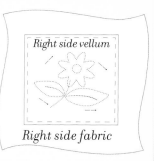

Right side vellum

Right side fabric

4. Use a quilt pounce, a tightly rolled piece of felt tied with a rubber band dipped in pounce powder, or a self-sticking felt circle dipped in pounce powder to carefully rub the powder over the motif. Less is more for this step. Once the entire design has been pounced, remove the pins and pattern.

Tip: Lightly tap the pouncing tool of choice so there is just a light coating of pounce powder on the tool.

5. Use the Sewline Trio Marking Pen or Pigma Micron .05 pen to draw over the pounced dots. When the motif is fully traced, give the fabric a few good shakes to remove the pounce powder.

6. Embroider the design with the Backstitch (page 50), Chain Stitch (page 56), or Stem Stitch (page 70).

Transfer Paper

This method works best on lightweight to medium fabrics, such as silks and cottons. The markings on the fabric are very fine lines that are easily covered by your stitches. The only transfer paper I recommend to date is Loew-Cornell transfer paper. It is available in art supply and some craft stores. It does not smear or smudge and is less likely to fade or disappear while stitching.

1. Place the fabric on a hard flat surface. Lay the transfer paper carbon side down on the right side of the fabric and place the design on top of the transfer paper. If you are transferring a large design, pin the design in place.

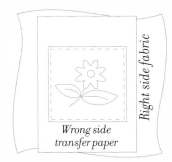

2. Trace the pattern design with the Sewline Trio Marking Pen using the tracer or stylus.

3. Remove the pattern design and transfer paper.

4. Embroider the design with the Backstitch (page 50), Chain Stitch (page 56), or Stem Stitch (page 70).

Transfer-Eze™

This method works well on washable fabrics. Once the design is stitched, it is rinsed in cold water to dissolve the Transfer-Eze. You will also need to stitch with colorfast threads to ensure they do not run when exposed to water. Transfer-Eze markings are an exact copy of the original pattern design and the pattern is nicely secured to the fabric while stitching. The motifs on pages 134-143 can be photocopied onto the Transfer-Eze. The individual pattern designs may then be trimmed leaving ¼" of the Transfer-Eze around the motif and placed on the fabric for embroidery. Transfer-Eze is a pliable film and needles well.

Note: Please read all of the product instructions included with the Transfer-Eze before using.

1. Photocopy a design onto the Transfer-Eze. Trim the Transfer-Eze close to the design.

2. Peel the freezer paper backing away and place the Transfer-Eze on the right side of the fabric.

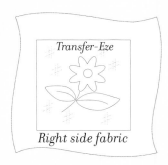

3. Embroider the design through the fabric and Transfer-Eze with the Backstitch (page 50), Chain Stitch (page 56), or Stem Stitch (page 70).

4. When your embroidery is finished, soak the block in cold water for 5-10 minutes to completely dissolve the Transfer-Eze. Soak longer if needed. Make sure the Transfer-Eze is thoroughly dissolved to keep your embroidered piece soft when dried.

Finishing the Block

Once a quilt top is pieced, it is typically sandwiched with batting and backing, quilted and bound. Crazy quilts are not traditionally sandwiched and quilted. If you have used a flannel foundation on your block it becomes the batting for the quilt. A backing is added and tack stitches are made at the block seam intersections to hold the top and backing together. No binding is required.

1. Using a ruler, mark an 18½" square on the right side of the embroidered top.

Note: The 18½" square may be outside the original marked and basted 18½" square due to shrinkage from the embroidery. It depends on the tightness of your stitches.

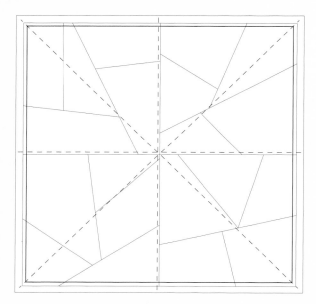

2. Machine stitch just inside the marked line all the way around the square. This will secure the hand embroidery when the block is trimmed to size.

Tip: Use a walking foot or even feed foot on the sewing machine to stitch the square.

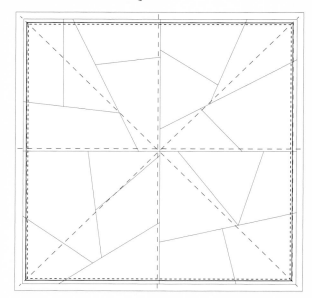

3. Trim the embroidered block to 18½". Remove any remaining basting stitches that held the block and flannel together prior to adding the embroidery.

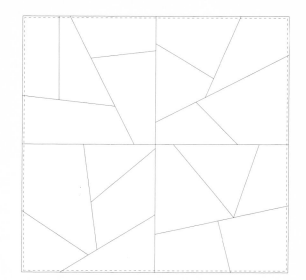

4. Layer the embroidered block and backing, right sides together. Stitch around the block leaving a 6" opening for turning.

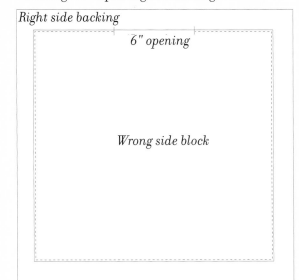

Right side backing

6" opening

Wrong side block

5. Turn the block right side out. Stitch the opening closed. Carefully press the outside edges rolling the backing to the back.

6. Tack stitch the top and backing together at the seam intersections as shown. These stitches will be hidden by the embroidery stitches.

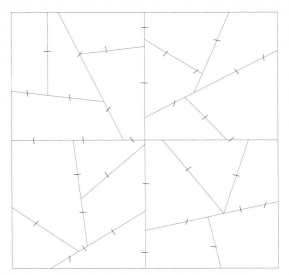

Tip: Add sparkle to the block by stitching a bead at the seam intersections when joining the block and backing together.

7. Place a label on the back of your block with your name, date, and location. Future historians will want to know who stitched this exquisite piece of needlework.

Note: Examples of the quilt labels from two of the projects in this book are shown.

I have included a few block samplers that were stitched by my students. Notice how each is unique to the stitcher. The stitch combinations and designs in this book give you numerous possibilities for making your blocks, projects and quilts personally distinctive.

Needle Artist: Elin Ely, Jacksonville, FL

Needle Artist: Marjorie Via, Jacksonville, FL

Needle Artist: Helen Anne Roesler, Jacksonville, FL

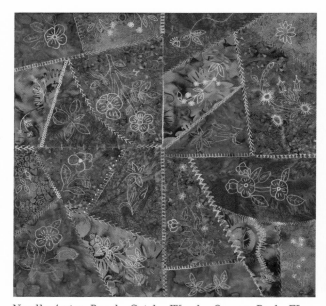

Needle Artist: Ronda Geisler Woods, Orange Park, FL

If you are interested in exploring more embellishing ideas, refer to *The Art of Elegant Hand Embroidery, Embellishment and Appliqué*. In this book, you will discover additional ribbonwork, stumpwork, and fabric techniques to further enhance your patchwork.

* ALL TEMPLATES ARE 100%
UNLESS NOTED OTHERWISE.
ADD ¼" SEAM ALLOWANCE.

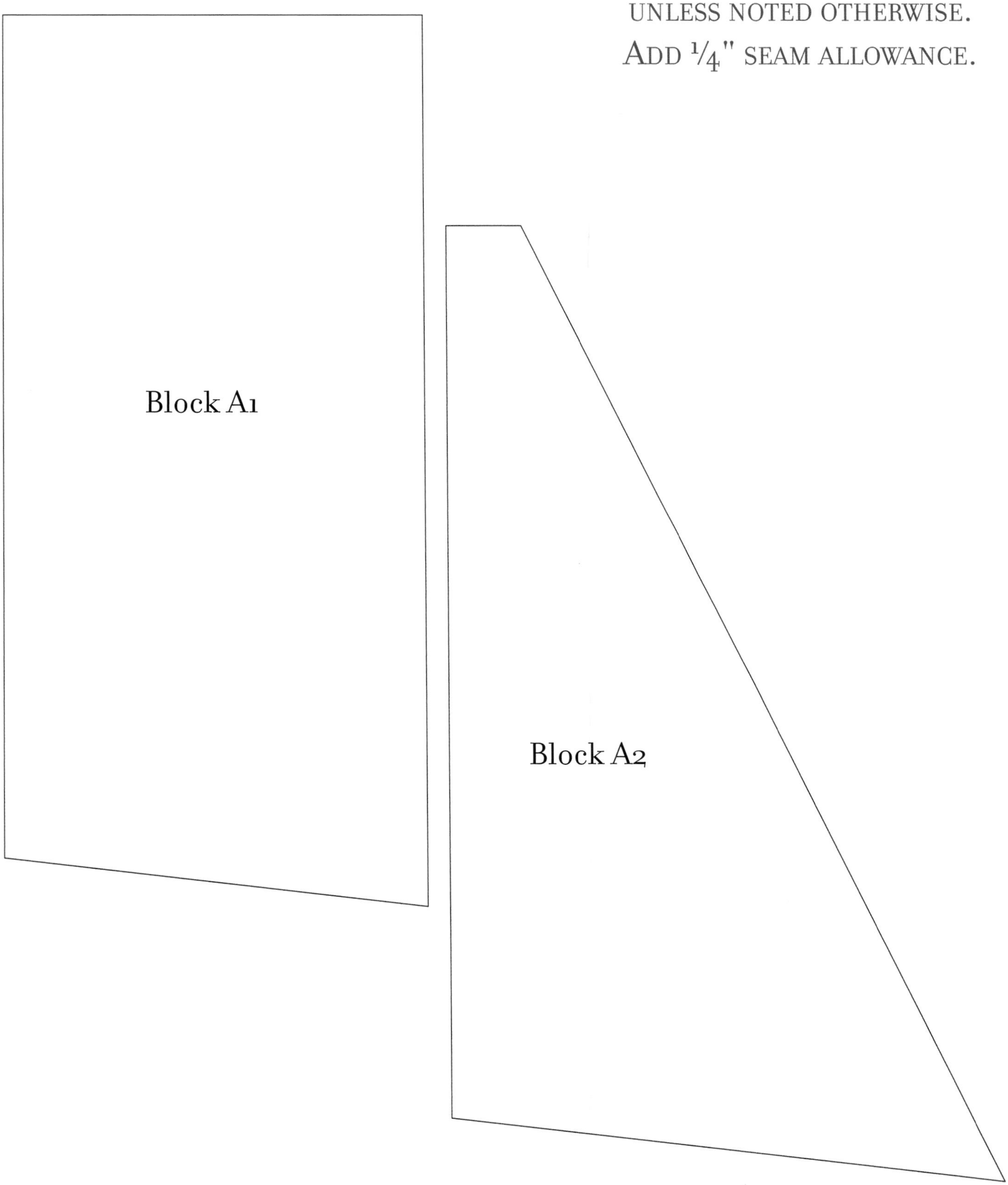

Block A1

Block A2

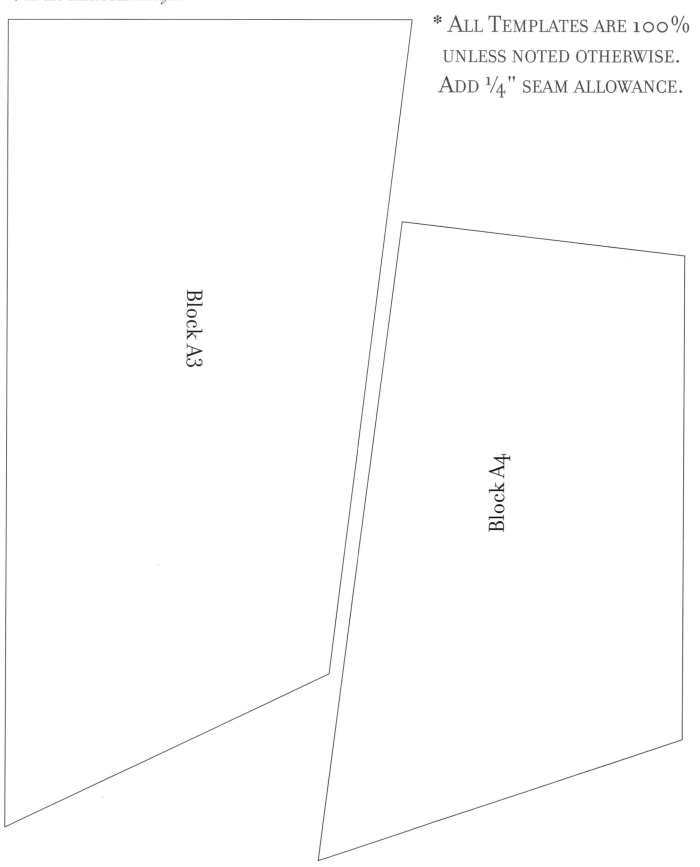

Block A3

Block A4

* ALL TEMPLATES ARE 100%
UNLESS NOTED OTHERWISE.
ADD $\frac{1}{4}$" SEAM ALLOWANCE.

* ALL TEMPLATES ARE 100%
  UNLESS NOTED OTHERWISE.
ADD ¼" SEAM ALLOWANCE.

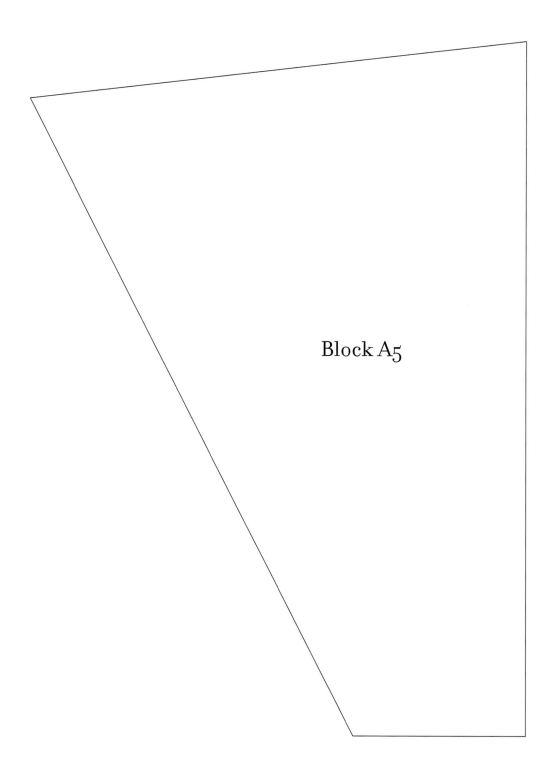

Block A5

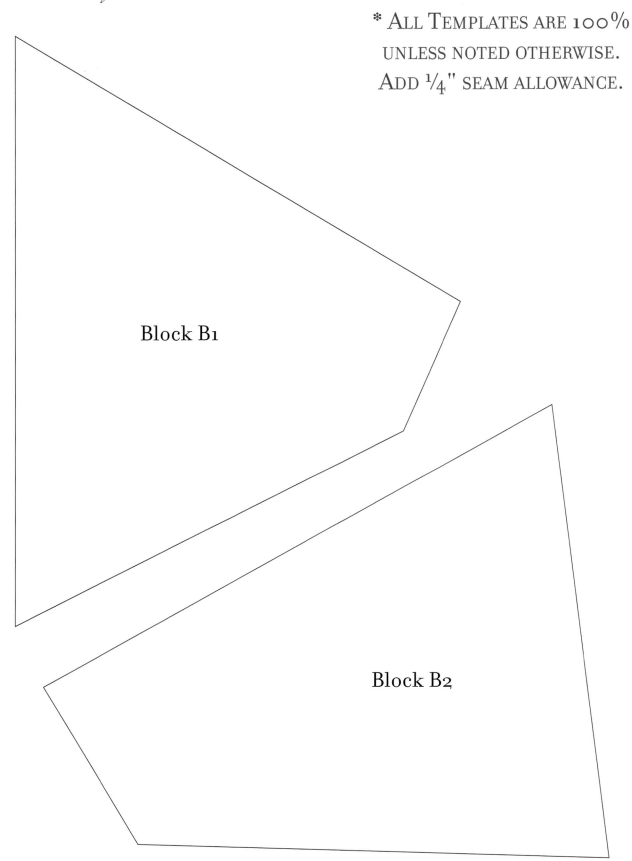

Block B1

Block B2

* ALL TEMPLATES ARE 100%
UNLESS NOTED OTHERWISE.
ADD ¼" SEAM ALLOWANCE.

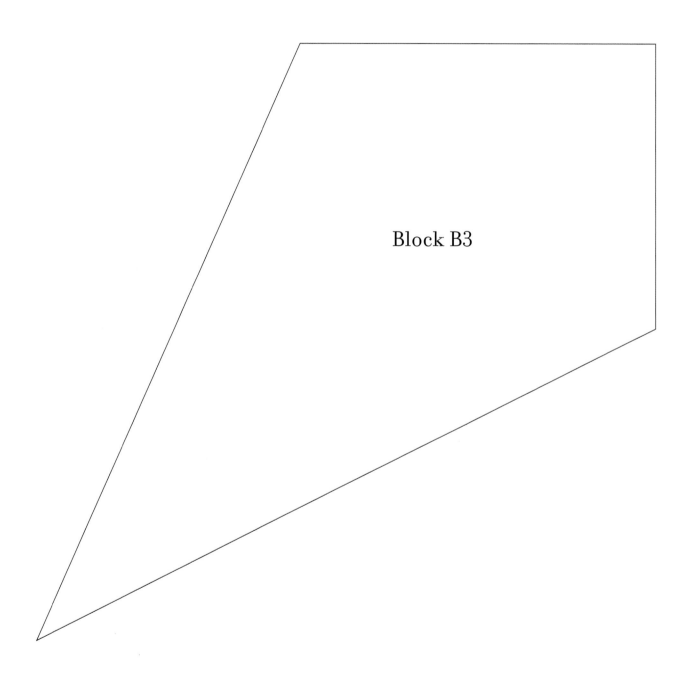

Block B3

*** ALL TEMPLATES ARE 100%
UNLESS NOTED OTHERWISE.
ADD ¼" SEAM ALLOWANCE.**

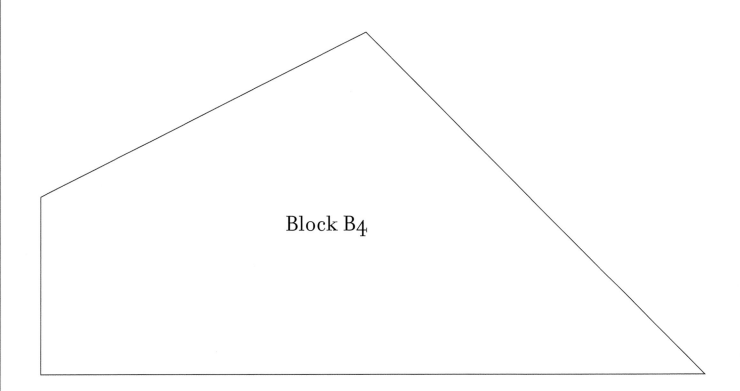

Block B4

* ALL TEMPLATES ARE 100%
  UNLESS NOTED OTHERWISE.
  ADD $\frac{1}{4}$" SEAM ALLOWANCE.

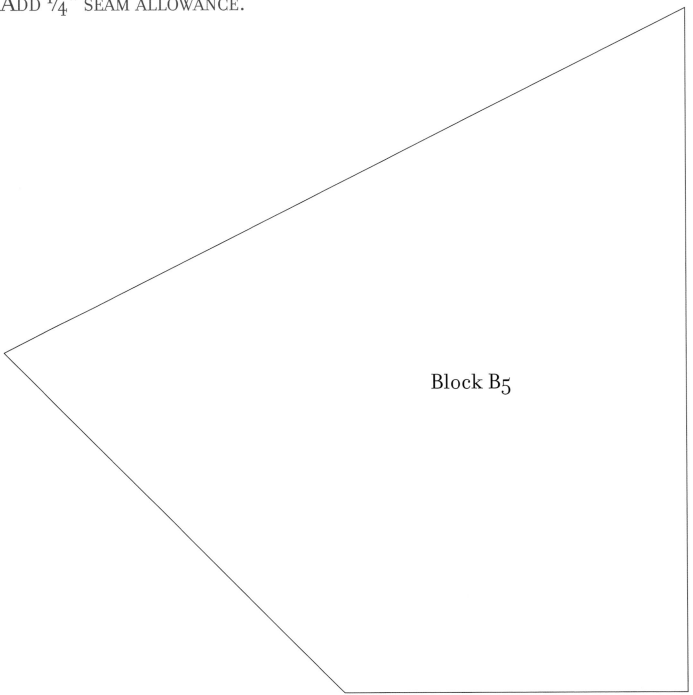

Block B5

* ALL TEMPLATES ARE 100%
  UNLESS NOTED OTHERWISE.
  ADD ¼" SEAM ALLOWANCE.

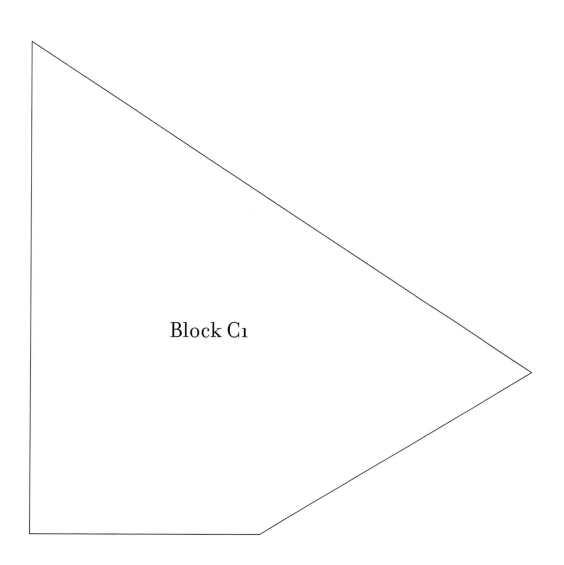

Block C1

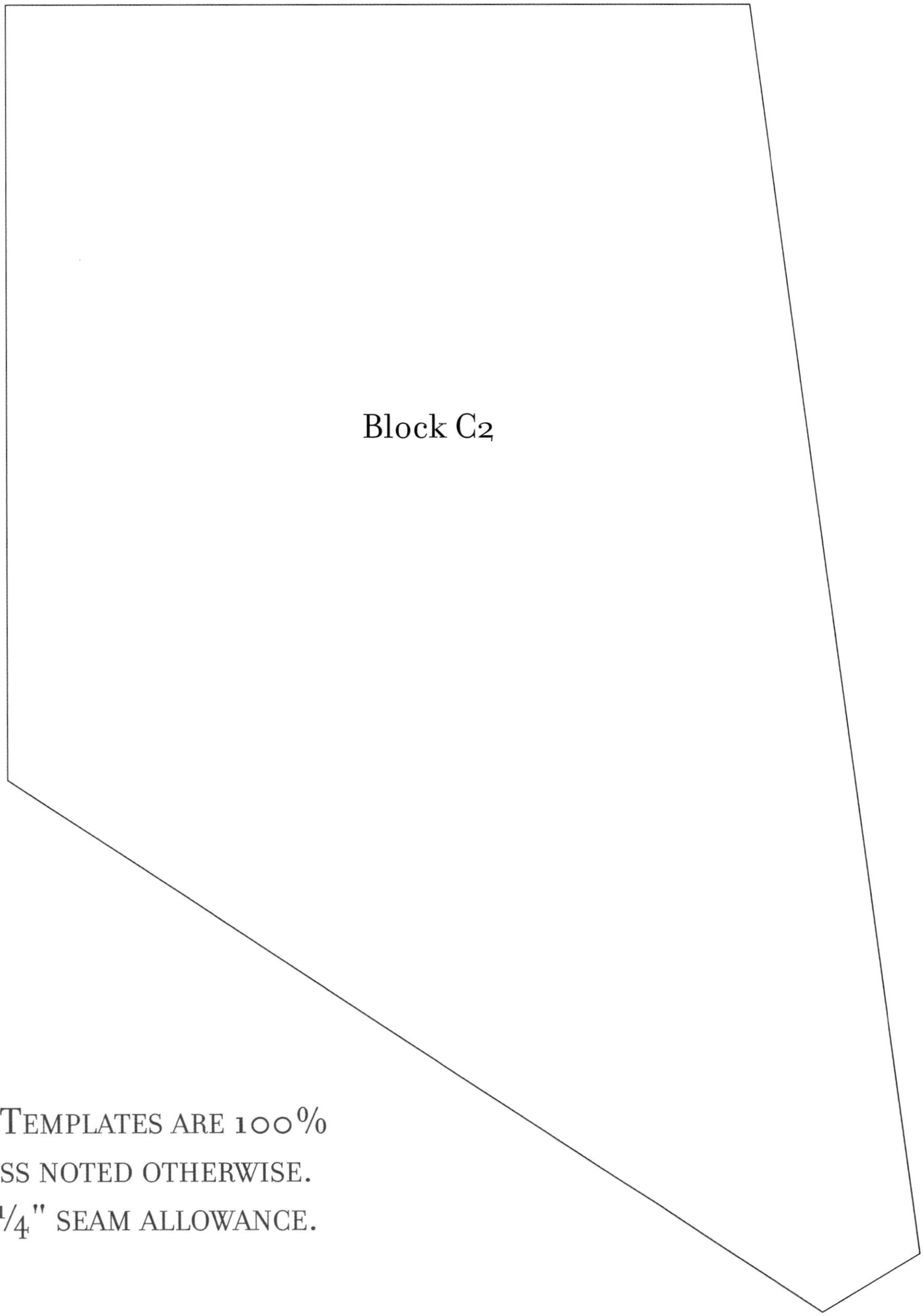

Block C2

* ALL TEMPLATES ARE 100%
UNLESS NOTED OTHERWISE.
ADD ¼" SEAM ALLOWANCE.

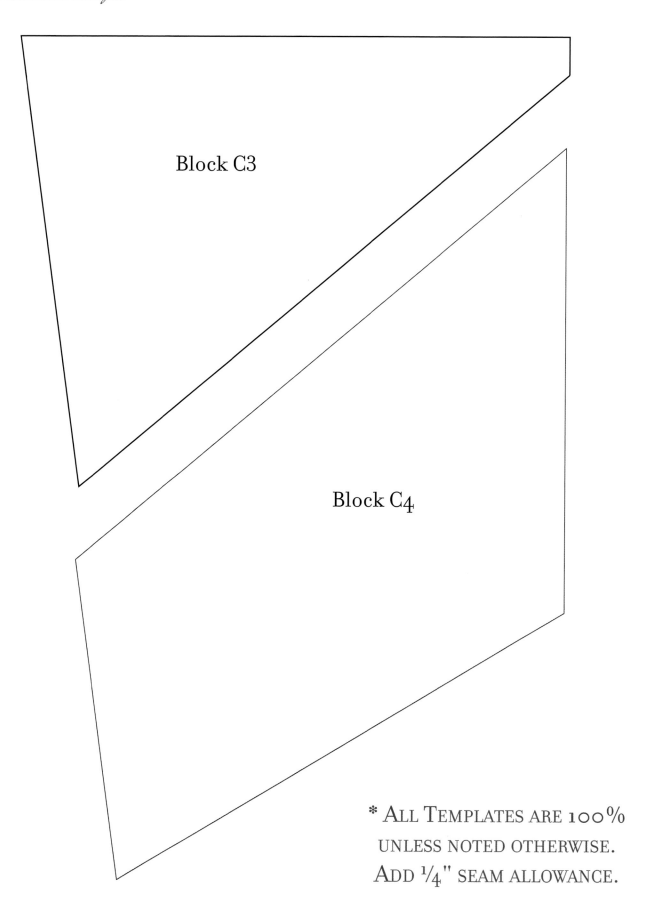

Block C3

Block C4

* ALL TEMPLATES ARE 100%
UNLESS NOTED OTHERWISE.
ADD ¼" SEAM ALLOWANCE.

* ALL TEMPLATES ARE 100%
UNLESS NOTED OTHERWISE.
ADD ¼" SEAM ALLOWANCE.

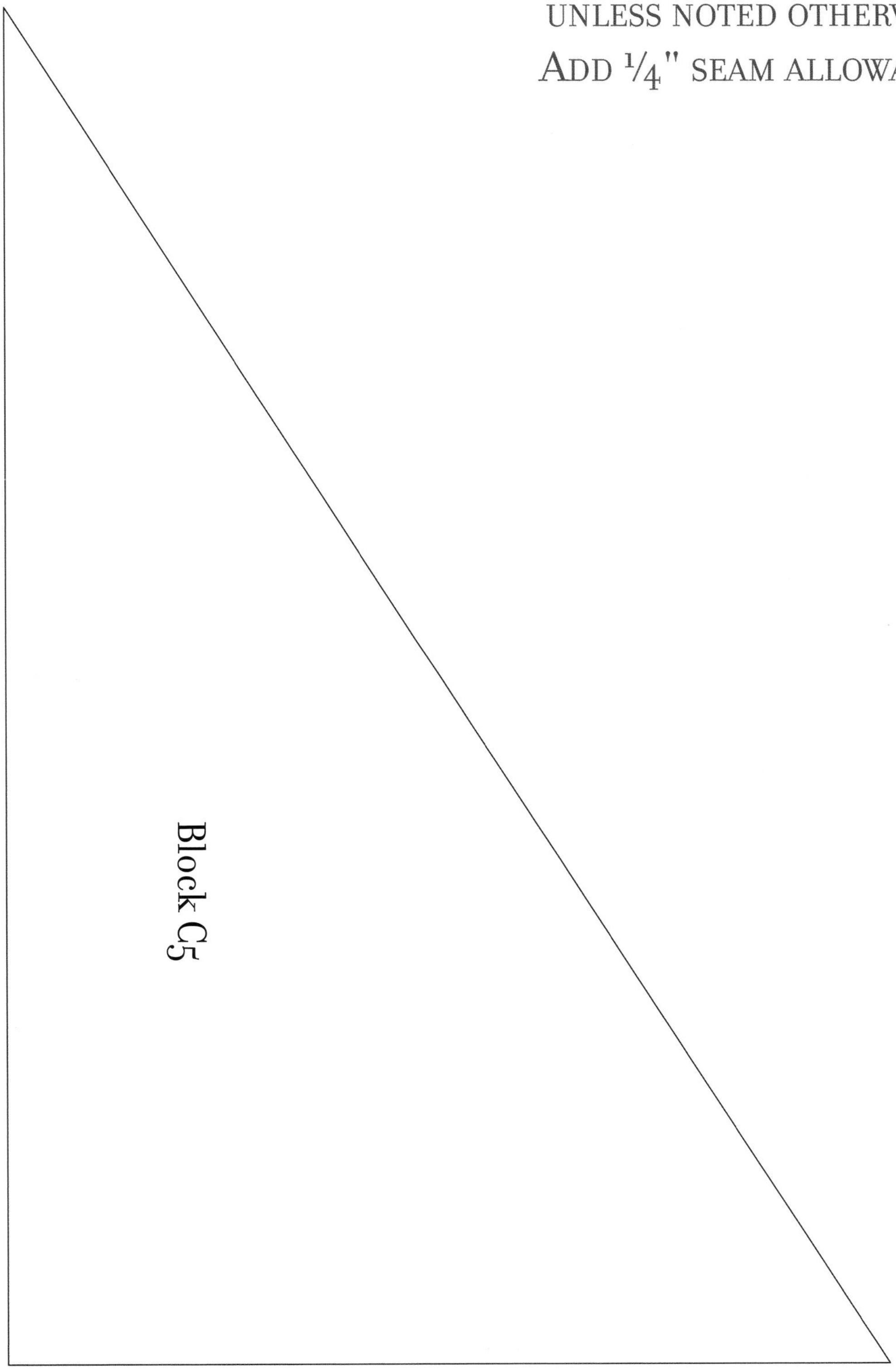

Block C5

* ALL TEMPLATES ARE 100%
UNLESS NOTED OTHERWISE.
ADD ¼" SEAM ALLOWANCE.

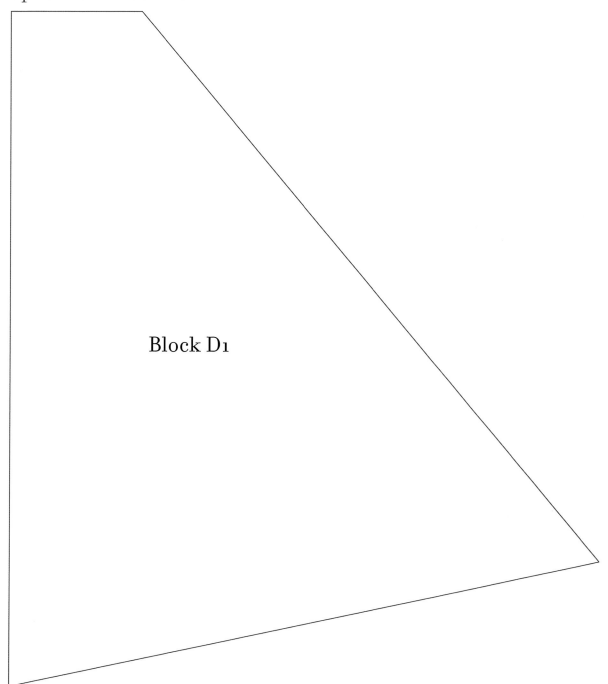

Block D1

* ALL TEMPLATES ARE 100%
UNLESS NOTED OTHERWISE.
ADD ¼" SEAM ALLOWANCE.

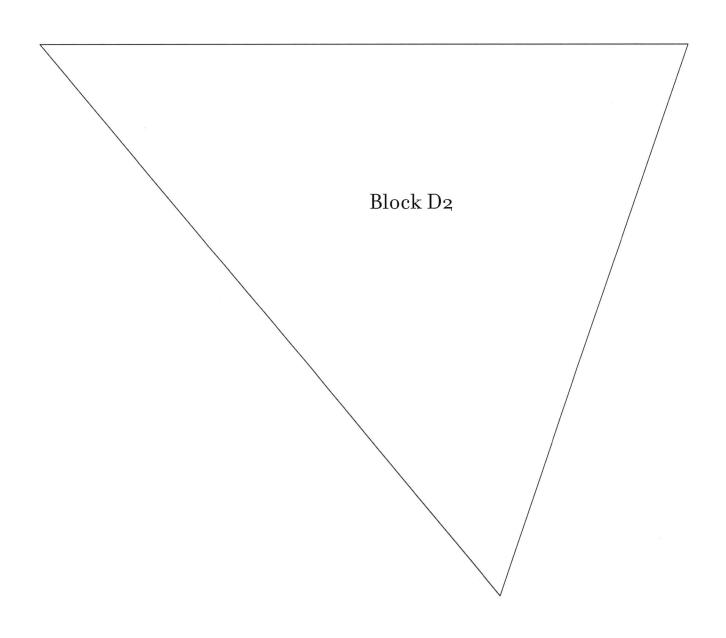

Block D2

* ALL TEMPLATES ARE 100%
UNLESS NOTED OTHERWISE.
ADD ¼" SEAM ALLOWANCE.

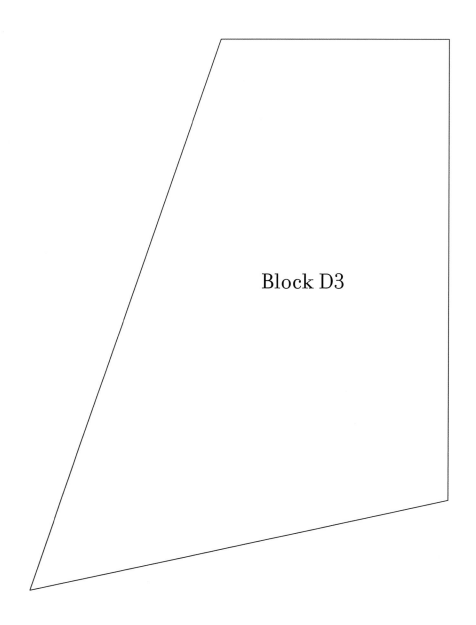

Block D3

* ALL TEMPLATES ARE 100%
  UNLESS NOTED OTHERWISE.
  ADD ¼" SEAM ALLOWANCE.

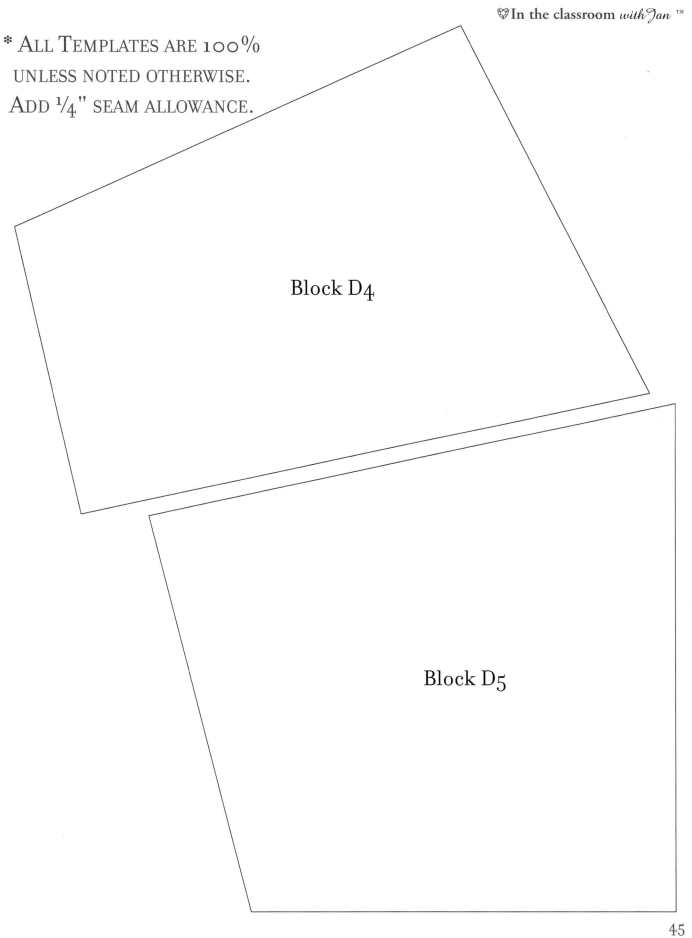

Block D4

Block D5

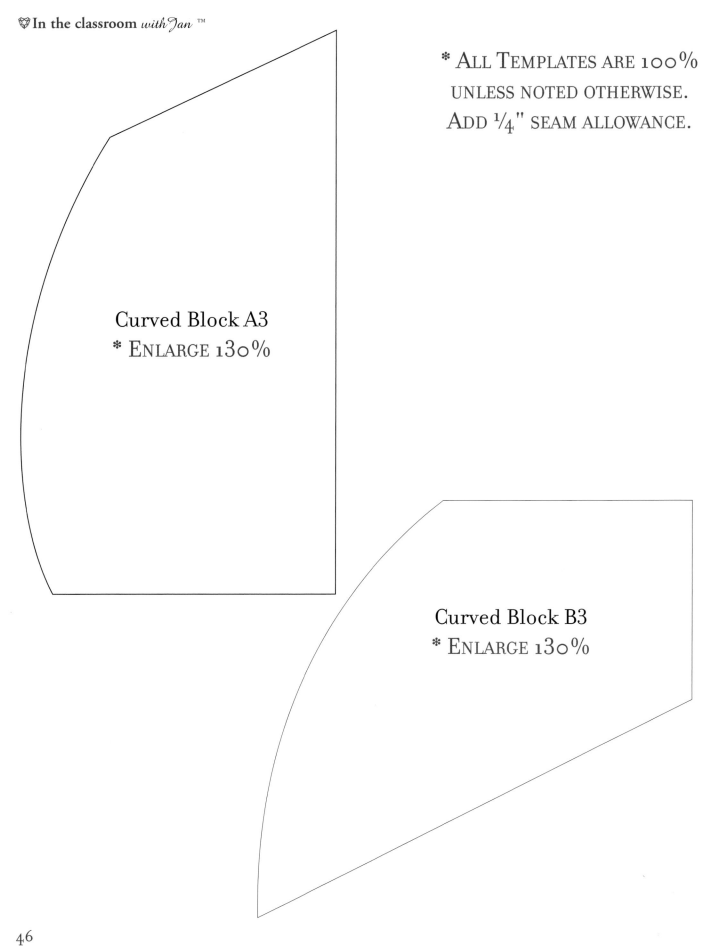

* ALL TEMPLATES ARE 100%
UNLESS NOTED OTHERWISE.
ADD ¼" SEAM ALLOWANCE.

Curved Block A3
* ENLARGE 130%

Curved Block B3
* ENLARGE 130%

* ALL TEMPLATES ARE 100%
UNLESS NOTED OTHERWISE.
ADD ¼" SEAM ALLOWANCE.

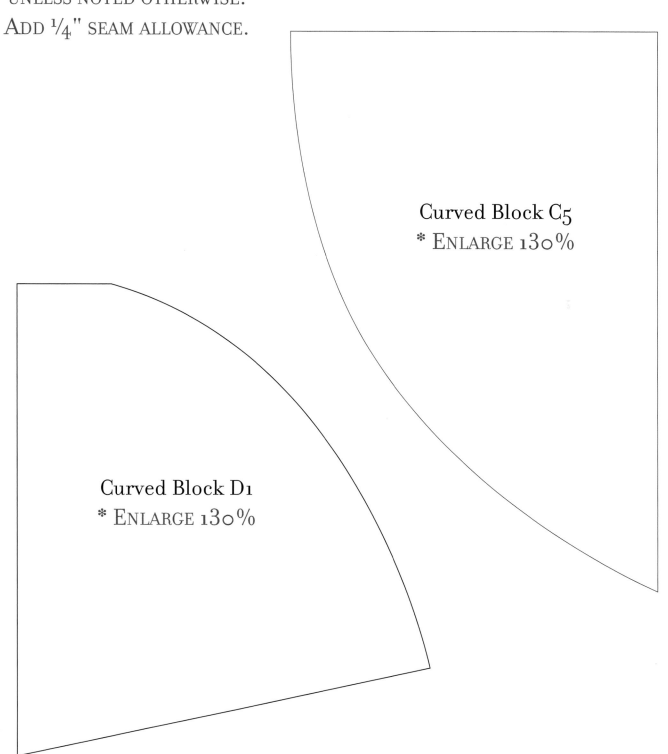

Curved Block C5
* ENLARGE 130%

Curved Block D1
* ENLARGE 130%

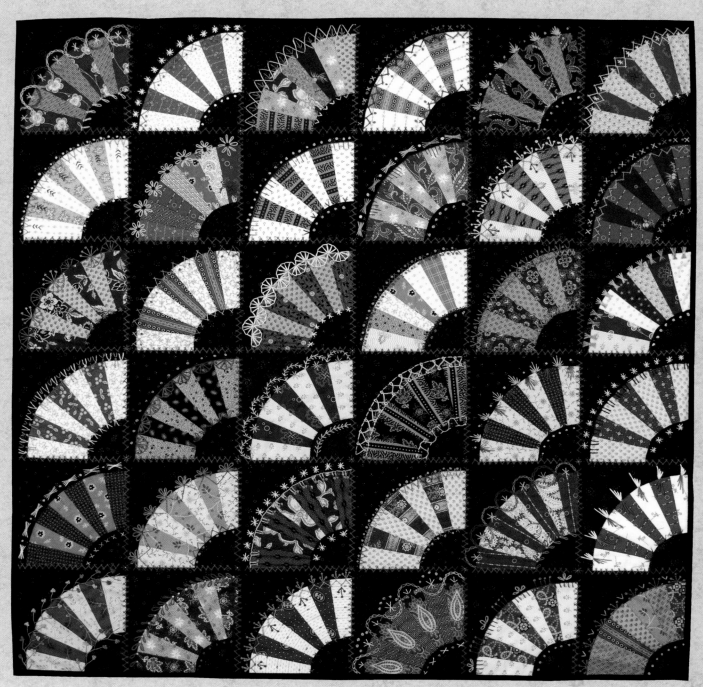

Fan Favorite

The Stitches

"There is today a real need for a book in which women will find the inspiration and the guidance to explore the possibilities of contemporary embroidery, a book in which stitches are so clearly and completely described that anyone can master them with little effort. The purpose of this book is to fill this need— to teach many stitches and to show how to work them into an attractive contemporary sampler." *The Stitches of Creative Embroidery*, by Jacqueline Enthoven

This quote is borrowed from Jacqueline's book published in 1964. Fifty years later the words are still fresh and pertinent. The contemporary samplers Jacqueline offered her readers were rows of stitches, a personal stitch encyclopedia they could refer to again and again. They were an opportunity for stitchers to express their creativity in color and with stitch combinations and variations.

This chapter of stitches allows you to be spontaneously creative once you have learned the mechanics of the stitch. You will soon learn that the most dramatic results can be obtained with the simplest of stitches. May you experience the joy of creating with these stitches.

Backstitch

The Backstitch is particularly suited to fine lines and details. It can be highly decorative by itself or in combination with other stitches.

The length of the stitch is determined by the thread or ribbon being used. The finer the thread, the shorter the stitch; the thicker the thread, the longer the stitch. Experiment with different threads and ribbons for the look you wish to create.

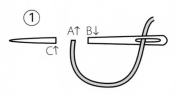

1. Bring the needle and thread to the front at A, approximately ⅛" from the beginning of the stitching line. This distance is the stitch length. Take the needle to the back at B, which is the beginning of the stitch line. Re-emerge approximately ⅛" beyond A at C. Pull the needle and thread through the fabric to complete the stitch.

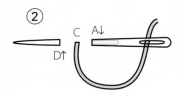

2. Take the needle to the back at A in exactly the same hole. Re-emerge at D, ⅛" from C. Pull the needle and thread through the fabric to complete the stitch.

3. Continue working stitches following step 2. To end, take the needle and thread through the hole at the beginning of the previous stitch (E) and secure on the back.

STITCH OPTION:
Use a quilting stencil design, such as the clamshell pattern, and Backstitch with Perle cotton to add texture to fabric.

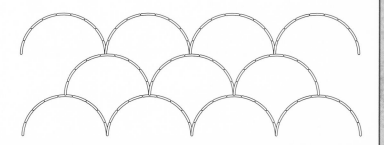

Blanket/Buttonhole Stitch

The Blanket Stitch and the Buttonhole Stitch are formed exactly the same. The difference is the distance between the vertical stitches. When there is spacing between the vertical stitches it is considered a Blanket Stitch. This stitch was used around the edges of a blanket adding strength and in some cases a decorative edge.

When the vertical stitches lay next to each other, or side by side, it is considered a Buttonhole Stitch. This stitch was used to reinforce the opening of a buttonhole adding strength and a finished edge.

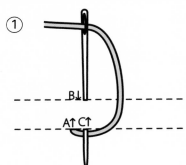

1. The stitch is worked from left to right over two imaginary horizontal lines. Bring the needle and thread up at A on the imaginary lower line. Take the needle down at B on the imaginary upper line and out at C on the imaginary lower line. Keep the working thread under the tip of the needle.

2. Pull needle and thread through the fabric forming a loop.

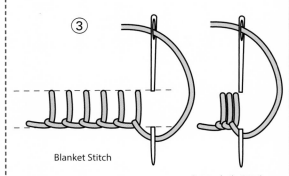

3. Continue making the vertical BC stitches with the working thread under the tip of the needle on each stitch.

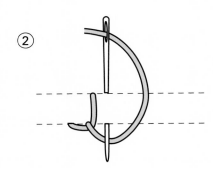

Blanket Stitch

Buttonhole Stitch

4. To end, take the needle and thread to the back at D and secure.

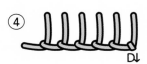

So much can be done using this wonderful knot. By varying the threads, length of the stitch, number of threads, or the number of wraps, the finished stitches are too numerous to list. From buds to flowers, sepals, petals, and leaves, even butterflies, caterpillars, and snails, the possibilities are endless.

It is best to work this stitch with a Straw or Milliner's needle since it has a consistent width the length of the needle shaft. This needle makes it easier to pull the working thread through the wraps. If using crewel wool, gimp, or ribbon, a Chenille needle is suggested for its wider eye, easily accommodating the thickness of these mediums.

①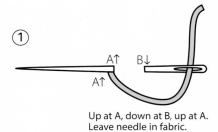

Up at A, down at B, up at A.
Leave needle in fabric.

1. Bring the needle and thread to the front at A, then to the back at B (horizontally right of A). Bring the tip of the needle to the front again at A. Do not pull the needle all the way through the fabric at this stage.

②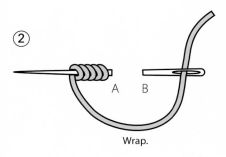

Wrap.

2. Gently wind the thread around the needle. These are referred to as "wraps". The number of wraps should cover the distance between A and B.

③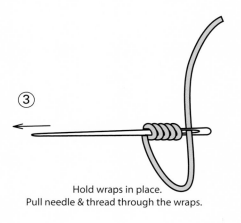

Hold wraps in place.
Pull needle & thread through the wraps.

3. Holding the wraps against the surface of the fabric with your thumb, gently pull the needle and thread through the wraps, placing the wraps on the working thread. Be sure the wraps lay side by side on the top of the fabric. These wraps should cover the space between A and B.

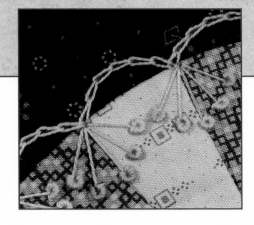

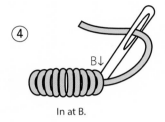

4. Take the needle to the back at B. The bullion should lay smoothly next to the fabric.

In at B.

Tip: In order to obtain a gentle curve to your bullion stitches the number of wraps should be greater than the distance between A and B. If 5 wraps nicely fill the space between A and B, add an additional 3-4 wraps for a curved effect between A and B. The gentle curve is useful for rosebuds and rose petals.

STITCH OPTIONS:
Make a bullion with 12 wraps with a distance between A and B of ¹⁄₁₆". This will make a Bullion Loop. Adjust the number of wraps based on the type of thread used and the size of the loop desired.

Make seven elongated Straight Stitches (page 73) of varying heights. Top each Straight Stitch with a Bullion Loop. See an example of this combination stitch from the center medallion block on page 105.

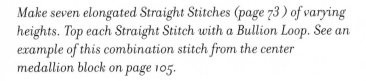

The Long and Short Buttonhole Stitch is a simple variation of the Blanket/Buttonhole Stitch. This multi-purpose stitch can be changed by applying different lengths and combinations to the vertical stitches. Here the variations are shown with straight lines, but it works equally well as circles for flowers or ovals for leaves.

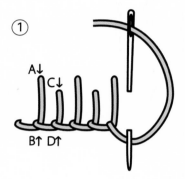

1. Referring to Blanket/Buttonhole Stitch steps 1-4 on page 51, alternate making one long vertical stitch (A to B) and one short vertical stitch (C to D). Alternate between the long and short vertical stitches to form the stitch line.

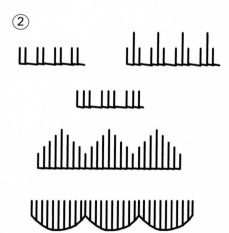

2. Vary the length, spacing, and number of vertical stitches for a variety of effects.

Buttonhole Stitch, Up and Down

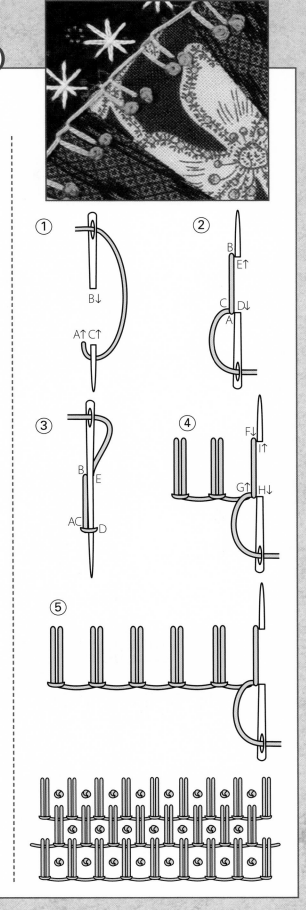

This variation of the Buttonhole Stitch adds a beautiful accent and makes a rich looking edging.

Tip: Work with Perle cotton 5 to learn the stitch.

1. Bring the needle and thread up at A. Take the needle down at B and up at C, close to A, with the working thread under the tip of the needle.

2. Pull the needle and thread through. Take the needle down at D, close to C, and straight up at E, close to B. Pull the needle and thread through.

3. Slip the tip of the needle down under the small horizontal bar between CD and draw the needle and thread through. This is the first pair of parallel stitches.

4. For the second pair of parallel stitches, move a little farther to the right. Take the needle down at F and up at G, with the working thread under the tip of the needle. Pull the needle and thread through. Take the needle down at H, close to G, and up at I, close to F. Pull the needle and thread through.

5. Slip the tip of the needle down under the small horizontal bar between GH and draw the needle and thread through. Continue working parallel pairs of stitches the desired length following steps 4-5.

Tip: The Up and Down Buttonhole Stitch was used frequently in the antique quilt that inspired this book, using both a double and triple effect. Get the effect of a Feather Stitch by alternating the straight stitches down and up, or side to side.

STITCH OPTION:
Overlap rows of the Up and Down Buttonhole Stitch. Fill in the spaces between the pairs of stitches with a Colonial Knot (page 59).

The Chain Stitch is a basic embroidery stitch that is quite versatile. It may be used for outlining or as a filling stitch. It makes beautiful stems or branches when rows are stitched side by side. Experiment with different thread mediums to acquire the look and texture desired for the design elements.

①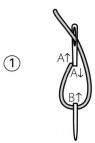

1. Bring the needle and thread to the front at A. In a downward stitch, insert the needle back down at A and out at B. Loop the working thread under the tip of the needle.

②

2. Pull the needle and thread through the fabric until the loop nestles around the emerging thread. Take the needle back down at B and out at C. Loop the working thread under the tip of needle. Pull the needle and thread through the fabric until the loop nestles around the emerging thread and forms a second loop.

③

3. Continue working stitches for desired length. To end, take the needle and thread to the back of fabric at D just below the last loop and secure.

Tip: Be careful not to pull the loops too tight or they will lose their rounded shape

Chain Stitch, Detached

A single Chain Stitch, also known as a Detached Chain Stitch or a Lazy Daisy Stitch, may be worked in a circle to form a flower that resembles a daisy, hence the name Lazy Daisy Stitch.

1. Bring needle and thread to the front at A. Take the needle down at A and out at B. Loop the working thread under the tip of the needle.

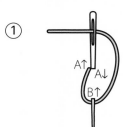

2. Pull the needle and thread through the fabric holding the loop in place with your thumb. Keep in mind the tighter you pull, the thinner the loop will become. Take the needle and thread to the back at C below the base of the loop to complete the Chain Stitch, Detached.

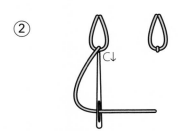

STITCH OPTIONS:

Group eight Detached Chain Stitches (petals) together in a circle. Add Colonial Knots (page 59) in the center of the petals to create a dainty little daisy.

Add stitches in the center of the Detached Chain Stitches such as a Bullion (page 52), an additional Detached Chain Stitch or a Straight Stitch (page 73) in different colors or threads to lend interest and dimension to the petals.

Vary the length of the finishing stitch of the Detached Chain Stitch to create a wildflower. Add a Colonial Knot (page 59) at the tip of each chain for interested.

Chain Stitch, Heavy

The Heavy Chain Stitch, also referred to as the Braid Stitch, is a beautiful decorative stitch. Work with a single thread or use a double thread to give the stitch a defined braided appearance. It is best to use a Tapestry needle with this stitch. The stitch works curves nicely.

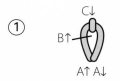

1. Bring the needle and thread to the front at A. Take the needle down at A and out at B with the working thread under the tip of the needle. Take the needle and thread down at C. The B-C stitch anchors the upside down Detached Chain Stitch (page 57).

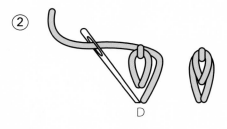

2. Bring the needle and thread up at D. Slide the needle and thread from right to left under the anchor stitch (B-C). Do not pierce the fabric or Chain Stitch. Take the needle and thread down at D.

3. Bring the needle and thread up at E, just below D. Slide the needle from right to left under the first and second Chain Stitches. Do not pierce the fabric. Take the needle and thread down at E.

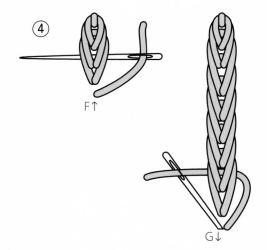

4. Continue working the Heavy Chain Stitch, coming up below the last chain. Slide the needle from right to left under the two previous Chain Stitches, then take the needle and thread down where the thread came up. To end, take the needle and thread to the back at G and secure.

Colonial Knot

The Colonial Knot, also known as the Candlewicking Knot, is similar in appearance to the French Knot and can be worked alone or to fill a shape. It is easier to work this stitch with the fabric in a hoop. This leaves your hands free to position stitches and to wrap the thread around the needle.

1. Bring the needle and thread to the front at A. Make a backward "C" with the thread. Place the tip of the needle under the top of the "C" close to A.

2. Lay the thread from the end of the "C" over the tip of the needle and shorten the loop around the needle.

3. Take the working thread under the tip of the needle. The thread looks like it is forming an almost closed figure 8.

4. Take the tip of the needle to the back at B, two threads away from where the thread originally emerged at A. Pull the wrapped thread firmly against the fabric and pull the needle and thread through to the back.

Tip: When pulling the needle and thread to the back, hold the knot and loop of thread on the fabric with your thumb until the knot lays on top of fabric.

STITCH OPTIONS:
The Colonial Knot adds dimension to any design and interest to single stitches. See Stitch Options for the Chain Stitch, Detached (page 57), Feather Stitch (page 63), Fly Stitch (page 64), and Stem Stitch, Sharp Corners and Joining Stitching Lines (page 72).

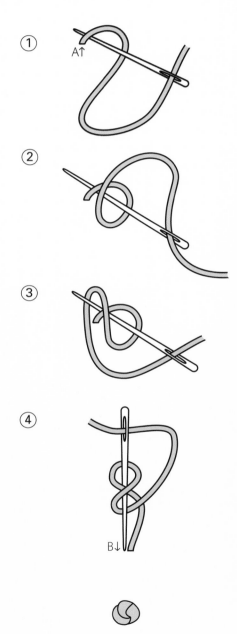

The Cross Stitch is a traditional and well-known embroidery stitch used to adorn clothing, home furnishings, and church vestments. It is typically worked on an even-weave fabric, such as linen or Aida cloth with a Tapestry needle while counting threads. It can be equally beautiful on other fabrics when worked on imaginary parallel lines.

The Cross Stitch is worked in rows, stitching the bottom half of the stitches from left to right and then working the top half of the stitches from right to left.

①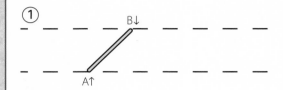

1. When working the Cross Stitch on fabric without an even weave, imagine you are stitching between two parallel lines. Beginning on the bottom left side of the line of stitching, bring the needle and thread to the front at A. Take the needle and thread to the back at B making a diagonal stitch. This is the first half of the first stitch.

②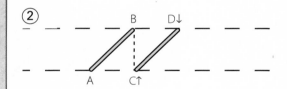

2. Bring the needle and thread to the front at C, directly below B and parallel to A. Take the needle and thread down at D parallel to B. This is the first half of the second stitch.

③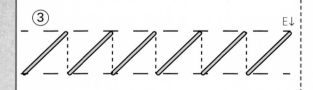

3. Continue working across the line of stitching, working the diagonal stitches bottom to top, left to right. Finish the bottom half of the stitches by taking your needle and thread down at the top of the last stitch (E).

Note: Each of the diagonal stitches are referred to as half cross stitches.

Cross Stitch

4. The top half of the Cross Stitches are worked from right to left. Bring the needle and thread to the front on the bottom line at F directly below the end of the last stitch (E). Take the needle and thread down diagonally at G in the same hole of the top of the next stitch.

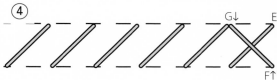

5. Bring the needle and thread to the front at H directly below G. Take the needle and thread down diagonally at I in the same hole of the top of the next stitch. Continue working across the row, diagonally crossing the bottom half of each cross stitch.

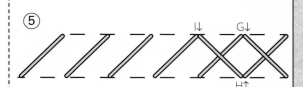

6. Finish the top half of the stitches by taking the needle and thread down at J directly above A, the beginning of your first stitch. Secure the stitch.

STITCH OPTIONS:

Work a double Cross Stitch by stitching one Cross Stitch with diagonal stitches, and one Cross Stitch with horizontal and vertical stitches on top of it. Add a third small Cross Stitch on each side of the vertical stitches to make a star.

Use different thread weights and colors to stitch the star for varying effects.

Feather Stitch

The Feather Stitch is a delicate stitch. It is adaptable and offers many variations. It may be worked with single feathers (or arms), double feathers and triple feathers. The Feather Stitch can vary in appearance depending on the thread, needle angle, and stitch length.

It is important to keep the thread tension, needle angle, and stitch length consistent to ensure even stitches. Stitch the Feather Stitch with a variegated or over-dyed thread for a pleasing effect.

①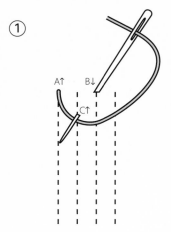

1. Use four imaginary lines to work this stitch. Bring the needle and thread to the front at A. Take the needle to the back at B and out at C with the working thread under the tip of the needle. Pull the needle and thread through the fabric forming a loop.

②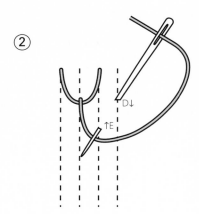

2. Pull the working thread toward the bottom, forming a "Y". Take the needle to the back at D and out at E with the working thread under the tip of the needle. Pull the needle and thread through the fabric forming a loop.

③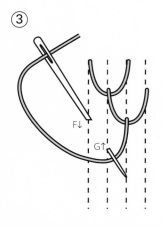

3. Pull the working thread toward the bottom, forming the second "Y". Take the needle to the back at F and out at G, with the thread under the tip of the needle. Pull the needle and thread through the fabric forming a loop.

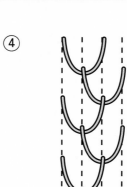

4. Repeat steps 2-3 for the desired length. To end take the needle and thread to the back at H and secure.

STITCH OPTIONS:

Interlace a row of Feather Stitches with a second row stitched in a different color or with a lighter value of the same color. Six-stranded cotton floss creates a rich effect.

Add a Colonial Knot (page 59) to the tip of each feather.

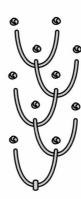

Fly Stitch

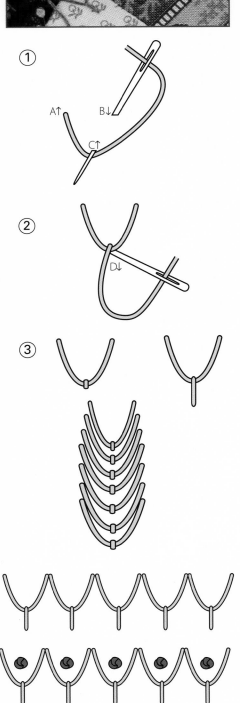

The Fly Stitch is another versatile stitch. It is often referred to as the "Y" stitch as it resembles the letter "Y". It is formed with a v-shaped loop fixed in place with a vertical Straight Stitch. The length of the Straight Stitch may be varied, changing the appearance and use of the stitch.

1. Bring the needle and thread to the front at A. Hold the thread down with the left thumb and insert the needle diagonally back into the fabric at B keeping it level and to the right of A. Bring the needle to front at C, with the working thread under the tip of the needle.

2. Pull the needle and thread through the fabric and position the loop to form a V shape. Take the needle to the back at D, forming a Straight Stitch to hold the loop in place.

3. A short or long Straight Stitch may be made, depending on the desired effect.

STITCH OPTIONS:

Work this stitch vertically stacked on top of each other. Stack the stitches close together to produce lacy leaf shapes.

Work the stitch horizontally placing the stitches side by side for a border effect.

Experiment with the Fly Stitch by using a different color thread to add another stitch in the center of the "Y", such as a Colonial Knot (page 59), a Cross Stitch Star (page 61) or a Bullion Loop (page 53).

Herringbone Stitch

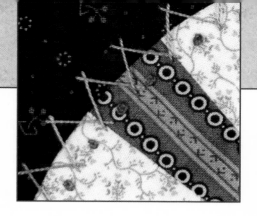

The Herringbone Stitch is a beautiful decorative stitch most often used to create borders. Visualize two parallel lines to keep your stitches evenly spaced.

1. Bring the needle and thread to the front on the lower line at A. With the working thread below the needle, take the needle down at B and up at C on the upper line.

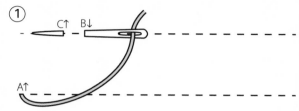

2. Pull the needle and thread through the fabric. With the working thread above the needle, take the needle down at D and up at E.

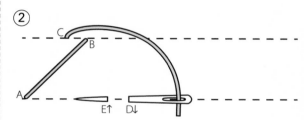

3. Pull the needle and thread through the fabric. Continue working stitches the desired length, evenly spacing and alternating stitches between the lower and upper lines.

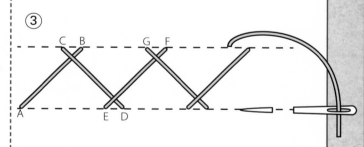

STITCH OPTIONS:

Space the stitches closer together or farther apart to acquire different effects.

Work a second row of Herringbone Stitches over the first, interlacing the stitches together. Working this second row with a different color thread highlights the decorative effect of the interlacing. The second color is laced under on the way up and over on the way down. In other words, ab passes under CD, cd over EF, ef under GH, gh over IJ, and so on.

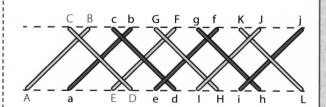

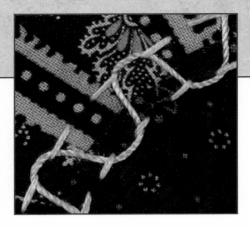

Interlaced Stitch

This stitch may be combined with a multitude of other stitches, such as the Backstitch, Chain Stitch, Fly Stitch, or Stem Stitch. Interlacing enriches the stitches adding dimension, color, or shading.

①

1. Stitch a line of Backstitches (page 50) or the stitch of your choice. These are the foundation stitches. The Interlaced Stitch combinations are only limited by your imagination.

②

2. Using a Tapestry needle, bring the needle and interlacing thread to the front at A centered below the first foundation stitch. Take the needle and thread up and under the second stitch, then down and under the third stitch. Do not pierce the fabric. The needle and thread are weaving through the foundation stitches. The interlacing thread may lay loosely on top of the foundation stitches forming loops or it may be gently pulled to nestle next to the foundation stitches.

③

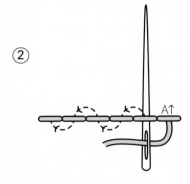

3. Continue weaving the thread up and down across the line of foundation stitches. At the end, take the needle and thread to the back at B centered below the last foundation stitch. Secure on the back.

STITCH OPTIONS:

A second row of Interlaced Stitches may be worked in and out in the opposite direction to form a series of loops on the top and bottom of the foundation stitches

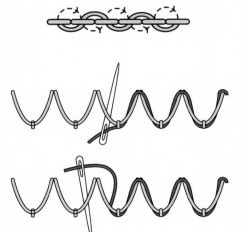

Interlace the Fly Stitch (page 64) with a secondary thread color.

Laced Cretan Stitch

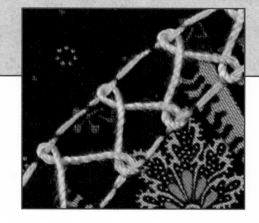

The Laced Cretan Stitch is also known as the Interlaced Backstitch. The stitch is interlaced over two parallel lines of backstitches.

1. Work two parallel lines of Backstitches (page 50). Offset the stitches on the top and bottom lines.

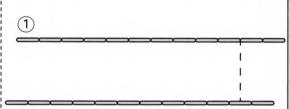

2. Using a Tapestry needle and working left to right, interlace the stitches, being careful not to pull the interlacing thread too tight. Working one stitch at a time and alternating from top to bottom, take the needle under the stitch. The working thread is under the needle. Pull the needle and thread through the stitch.

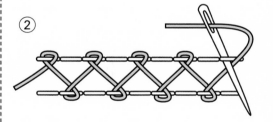

Note: When interlacing the stitches, the needle does not pierce the fabric. The stitches are interlaced through the stitches only.

STITCH OPTIONS:
If the Backstitches are small, the effect is a solid braid. If the stitches are larger, the effect is more open and airy.

Use two colors to work the Laced Cretan Stitch, one color for the Backstitches and another color to interlace the stitches.

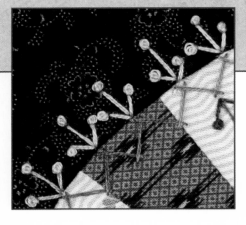

Pistil Stitch

The Pistil Stitch is a combination stitch made up of a French Knot on the end of a Straight Stitch. It is useful for making flower stamens, flower centers, or dainty flowers.

①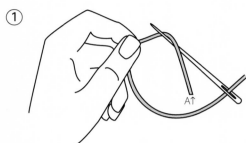

1. Bring the needle and thread to the front at A (the base of the Straight Stitch). Holding the working thread firmly with your left hand, bring the thread over the needle.

②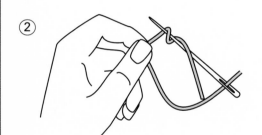

2. Wrap the working thread counterclockwise around the needle two times.

③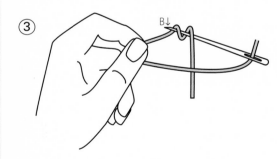

3. Holding the thread taut, place the tip of the needle in the fabric at B (the end of the Straight Stitch).

④

4. Slide the wraps down the needle onto the fabric. Pull the needle and thread to the back of the fabric to form the French Knot at the top of the Straight Stitch.

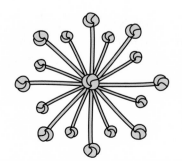

STITCH OPTION:
Stitch Pistil Stitches in a circle to make a delicate flower.

Sheaf Stitch

The Sheaf Stitch is made up of several Straight Stitches that are tied together horizontally in the middle. The stitch looks like sheaves of wheat, thus the name. The stitch is often used in rows for borders or in groups as a filling stitch.

1. Make three or four vertical Straight Stitches side by side and equal in length, with small spaces between them. Bring the needle and thread up at A and down at B, up at C and down at D, up at E and down at F, up at G and down at H.

2. Bring the needle and thread up at I, in the middle between CD and EF. Without piercing the fabric, slip the needle under CD and to the left of AB.

3. Take the needle and thread from right to left, over and under the four Straight Stitches, wrapping the thread around all four of the Straight Stitches.

4. Repeat twice, snugging the thread to pull the sides of the Straight Stitches into the middle. Take the needle and thread down at I and secure.

STITCH OPTIONS:

Vary the look of the stitch by moving the wraps toward the top of the Straight Stitches or down toward the bottom of the Straight Stitches.

Increase the number of Straight Stitches to tie together.

Make the Straight Stitches longer or shorter and increase or decrease the space between them. Experiment with these options on sample fabric to test for desired results.

Another variation of the Sheaf Stitch is made by stacking tepees of four Straight Stitches on top of one another. Run a line of Backstitches (page 50) down the middle of the apexes of the tepees.

①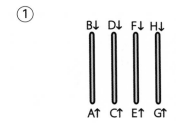

②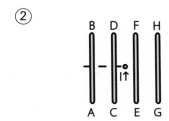

③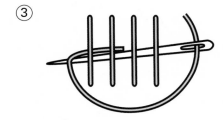

④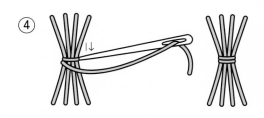

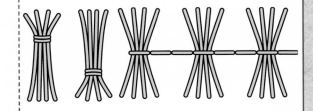

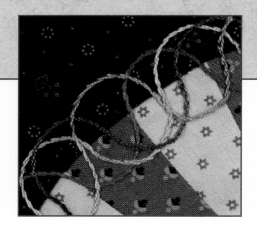

This stitch describes its purpose. Stitch several rows of Stem Stitches side by side to make a thicker stem for a flower or tiny branch. Experiment with 2, 3, or 6 strands of floss, Perle cotton, or gimp to see the beautiful effects this basic embroidery stitch has to offer.

①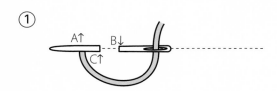

1. Bring the needle and thread to the front at the left end of the stitching line at A. With the working thread below the needle (swings low), take the needle to the back at B and up at C between A and B.

②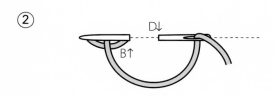

2. Pull the needle and thread through the fabric. Again with the thread below the needle (swings low), take the needle down at D (a stitch length away) and up at B. Pull the needle and thread through the fabric.

③

3. Following step 2 continue working stitches across the stitching line. Always keep the thread below the needle. To end, take the needle and thread to the back at E for the last stitch without re-emerging. Secure on back.

Tip: The Stem Stitch's working thread is below the needle, or swings low. This can be easily remembered by coupling the "S" for Stem Stitch and swing low or stay low.

Outline Stitch

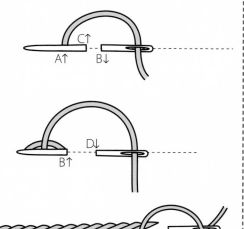

STITCH OPTIONS:
The Outline Stitch is worked in the same manner as the Stem Stitch, but the position of the working thread is different. In the Outline Stitch the working thread is above the needle or over the top. Couple the "O" for Outline Stitch and over the top.

Stem Stitch
Sharp Corners and Joining Stitching Lines

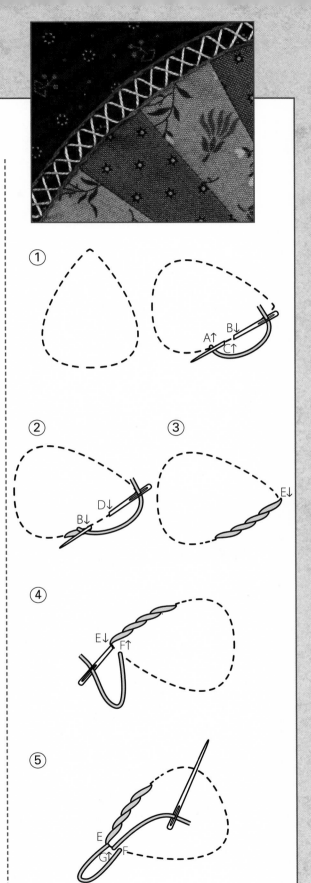

The Stem Stitch can be easily manipulated to make sharp corners for tips of leaves, stars, squares, or inside corners of scallops. It also fluidly joins lines of stitching to form smooth circles and scallops, or to outline shapes.

1. Lightly mark the desired shape on the fabric. Working the Stem Stitch from left to right, bring the needle and thread to the front at A. With the working thread below the needle (swings low), take the needle to the back at B and up at C between A and B.

2. Pull the needle and thread through the fabric forming the first stitch. With the thread below the needle (swings low), take the needle down at D and up at B.

3. Continue working stitches in the same manner to the corner (tip of leaf). Take the needle and thread to the back at E precisely in the corner (tip of leaf). You will need to judge the distance to the corner in order to make a full stitch into the corner.

4. Turn your work to begin working left to right on the second side of the leaf. Bring the needle and thread to the front at F, a stitch length away from the corner (tip of leaf). Take the needle and thread back down at E in the same hole where you ended the first side of stitching. Keep the working thread below the stitching line. Leave a loop below the stitching line.

5. Bring the needle to the front at G, in the middle of E and F. Pull the thread through, making the first stitch on the second side of the leaf.

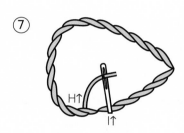

6. Continue working Stem Stitches around the leaf, turning your work as you stitch around the design. Join the lines of stitching by taking the needle and thread to the back at A in the same hole where you began stitching. This is the joining stitch.

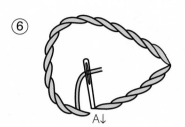

7. Bring the needle and thread to the front at H, just above the center of the joining stitch and down at I, centered underneath the first stitch made on the design. You now have an invisible joining stitch so the Stem Stitches form a continuous line of stitching. This joining method will work on circles or anywhere two lines of Stem Stitches come together.

Tip: On curved edges keep the length of your Stem Stitches shorter than on a straight line. This will hold the previous stitches in place making a neat, smooth curve or circle.

STITCH OPTION:
Stitch a serpentine with the Stem Stitch. Add Colonial Knots (page 59) in a contrasting color to the valleys.

Straight Stitch

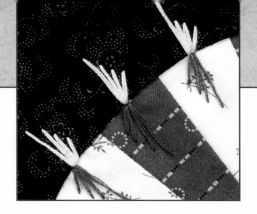

The Straight Stitch is the most basic of all embroidery stitches. It may be stitched in any length and worked in any direction, vertically, horizontally, or diagonally. It is the foundation of many embroidery stitches, and often combined with other stitches.

1. Bring the needle and thread to the front at A. Take the needle and thread to the back at B. One Straight Stitch is made.

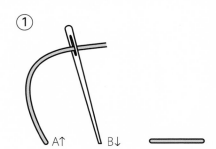

STITCH OPTIONS:

Alternate long and short Straight Stitches to form a star.

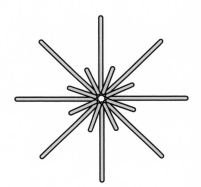

Sew Straight Stitches worked in a double circle with Colonial Knots (page 59) in the center to form a flower.

Make a Wild Flower with seven Straight Stitches in varying lengths, topped with a Bullion Loop (page 53).

Scrappy Tidbits

Useful Things

A quilt is a treasure and labor of love, especially a patchwork quilt complemented with myriads of embroidery stitches and motifs. However, if you like short-term gratification, it is nice to have the choice of a simple project or two. This chapter offers Useful Things that progressively build your confidence and skills, from a simple Étui to the antique-inspired A Quilt to Dream Under.

Étui

Needle Artist: Janice Vaine, Jacksonville, FL

Étui is French for a small decorative case used for needles, toiletry articles, or the like. Its first known use was between 1605-1615. Jump ahead to the 21st century and this precious Étui is as useful now as it was 400 years ago.

Finished size: 3½" x 11"

SUPPLIES:

- One fat quarter
- #18 Chenille needle
- #3 Perle cotton for edging
- Small amount of polyester stuffing
- 1 button
- 1" square of Velcro®

CUTTING INSTRUCTIONS:

- 2—4" x 15" strips for lining and front
- Use the Étui Curved Top Template to cut the curved flap edges on the lining and front strips.

GENERAL INSTRUCTIONS:

Seam allowances are ¼" unless otherwise noted.

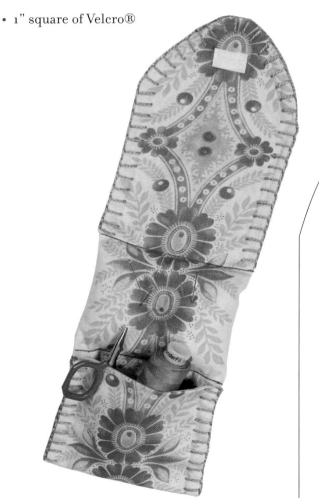

Étui Curved Top Template

¼" seam allowances are included.

Making the Étui:

1. Sew Velcro® to the lining and front fabric strips as shown.

2. Sew the lining and front, right sides together as shown, leaving a 2" opening for turning and stuffing the pincushion section. Trim the curved edge with pinking shears. Turn right side out and press.

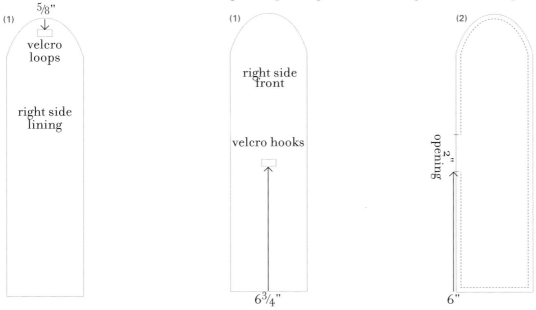

3. Double stitch the lines for the pincushion section as shown.

4. Stuff the pincushion section with a small amount of polyester stuffing. Turn the seam allowances to the inside at the opening and hand or machine stitch it closed.

5. Fold the bottom edge up 3" forming the inside pocket. The top of the pocket will be at the bottom of the pincushion section.

6. Join the front and back edges of the pocket with the Blanket Stitch (page 51) using #3 Perle cotton. Blanket Stitch the edges above the pincushion with the #3 Perle cotton.

7. Sew a button on the outside of the front flap, covering the stitching from the Velcro. Fold the pocket up onto the pincushion. Fold the flap with the Velcro loops over the pocket and pincushion and close with the Velcro hooks on the front.

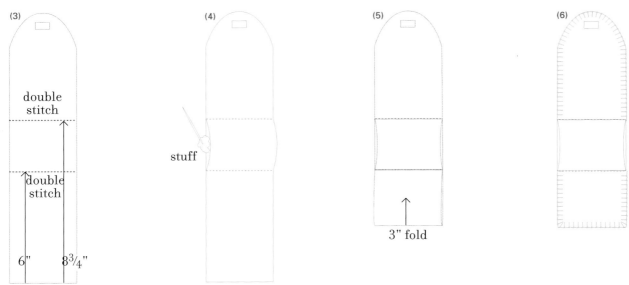

77

Finished size: 18" x 18" x 9"

Needle Artist: Luella Dusek, Pittsburgh, PA

Marquette Tote
A Textile Lover's Sampler

In France samplers were called "marquettes" and were functional rather than creative past-times. The samplers were mainly used as lessons to teach young girls how to embroider.

This project is both functional and creative. It's a great bag for classes or traveling with projects. It doubles as a stylish eco-friendly shopping bag, perfect for shop hops, quilt shows, or stopping at the market on your way home.

Creative stitching possibilities abound for the front and back of the tote. My mom, who embroidered the tote, artistically combined stitches and threads. She used a mixture of thread weights throughout the piece combining one to six strands of floss with Perle cotton 5, 8, and 12 weights. Solid and hand-dyed threads blend beautifully, as do flosses and crewel wools. Use this project to learn stitches and experiment with stitch and thread combinations.

FABRIC:

- Patchwork Blocks—Assorted cotton pieces and/or linen, silk, wool, and velvet
- Accent Fabric—1 yard
- Lining—1⅝ yards
- Cotton Flannel—1¼ yards

NOTIONS:

- 6-stranded embroidery floss in colors to complement and accent patchwork
- 1" cotton or poly belting—4 yards
- One large decorative button
- #100 Jeans needle

Optional:

- Four buttons to accent the sides of the tote
- Foam core—2—8" x 18" pieces joined together with double-stick tape

GENERAL INSTRUCTIONS

Seam allowances are ¼" unless otherwise noted. Press seams open. Read through In the Classroom with Jan™ on pages 8-30 before beginning.

CUTTING INSTRUCTIONS:

Patchwork Block Fabric:

- Refer to Cutting Instructions on page 12 and Block A-D templates on pages 31-47 to cut pieces for eight Patchwork Blocks

Accent Fabric:

- 2—10½" x width of fabric strips for Sides/Bottom Panel
- 5—2½" x width of fabric strips for binding
- 1—1" x 12" strip for button closure

Lining Fabric:

- 2—18½" squares for Front and Back
- 2—10½" x width of fabric strips for Sides/Bottom Panel
- *Optional:* 1—17½" x 21" for sleeve for foam core

Cotton Flannel:

- 2—20" squares
- 2—10½" x width of fabric strips. Piece the strips together and trim to 10½" x 56".

MAKING THE OUTER BAG:

Front and Back Sampler Blocks:

1. Use the cotton, linen, silk, wool and/or velvet to make eight patchwork blocks following the instructions on pages 13-19. Referring to page 21, sew the patchwork blocks together in sets of four to make two sampler blocks.

2. Place a sampler block right side up on a 20" flannel square. Baste the pieces together vertically, horizontally, and diagonally. Mark an 18½" square on the sampler blocks. Baste on the marked line. Repeat with the remaining sampler block and flannel square.

Make 2

EMBROIDERING THE SAMPLER BLOCKS:

1. Use the 6-stranded cotton floss and your choice of embroidery stitches from pages 50-73 to decorate the seams of the patchwork. Stitch to the edges of the marked 18½" square. This will ensure the stitches are secured in the seam allowance when the Marquette Tote is constructed. Remove the basting stitches as they intersect with the embroidery.

2. Choose floral motifs from pages 134-143 to embellish the patchwork.

3. Center and sew a decorative button 3½" from the top of the Sampler block you will be using as the front of your tote.

4. When the embroidery is complete, remove any remaining basting stitches. Trim each block to 18½" square.

MAKING THE LINING:

Handles

1. Cut two 64" lengths from the cotton belting. Fold one piece of the belting in half lengthwise to find the center and mark with a pin. Measure 2½" on either side of the center pin and mark with pins. Fold the marked section in half and stitch the edges together for 5". Repeat on the second piece of belting.

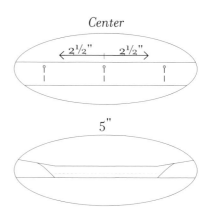

Center

2½"   2½"

5"

2. Place one handle on the right side of the front lining piece, 4½" from each side. Pin in place. Edge stitch the left side of the belting 16" up the front lining, across the top, and back down 16". Stitch an "X" in a 1" square at the top of the stitched belting. Repeat on the right side of the handle.

3. Stitch the second piece of belting on the right side of the back lining piece, referring to step 2.

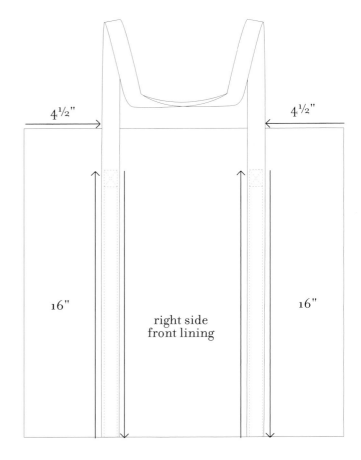

PUTTING IT ALL TOGETHER

1. Pin the front Sampler Block and front lining piece wrong sides together and baste. Pin the back Sampler Block and back lining piece wrong sides together and baste.

Tip: Be careful not to catch the handles in the basting stitches.

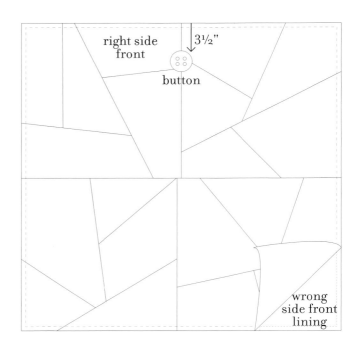

2. Sew the two Accent fabric Sides/Bottom Panel pieces together to form a long strip. Trim the pieced strip to 10½" x 56", centering the seam in the middle of the 56" strip. Repeat for the Lining Sides/Bottom Panel. Sandwich the Accent Sides/Bottom Panel, cotton flannel 10½" x 56" piece, and Lining Sides/Bottom Panel pieces together, right sides out. Hold in place with 505 Spray. Diagonally cross hatch the panel or quilt as desired. Trim the panel to 9½" x 54½".

Note: From this point forward, use the #100 Jeans needle in your sewing machine. You will be sewing through multiple layers and the Jeans needle will make it easier to stitch through the thickness.

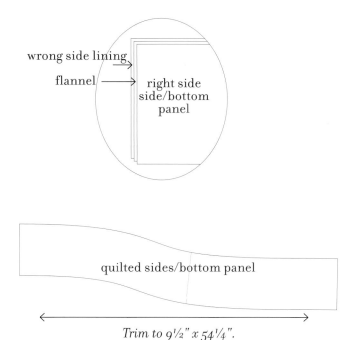

wrong side lining

flannel → right side side/bottom panel

quilted sides/bottom panel

Trim to 9½" x 54¼".

3. Pin the Sampler front to the quilted Sides/Bottom Panel wrong sides together along both sides of the tote. Baste both sides of the Front and Side/Bottom Panel together stopping ¼" from the bottom edge.

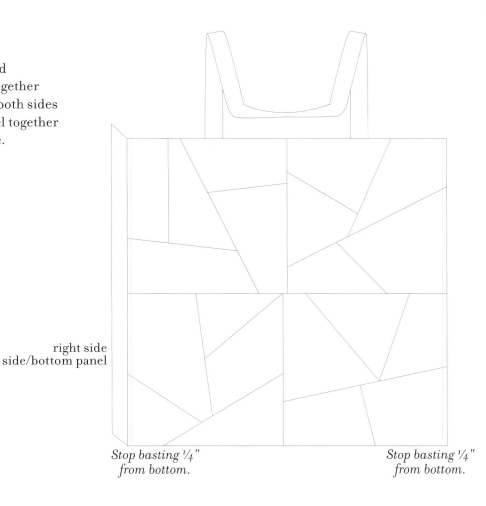

right side side/bottom panel

Stop basting ¼" from bottom.

Stop basting ¼" from bottom.

81

4. Pin the Sampler front to the Sides/Bottom Panel along the bottom edge, wrong sides together. Clip diagonally into the corner. Do not clip past the ¼" seam allowance. Baste the bottom edge stopping ¼" from the sides. Repeat steps 3 and 4 to attach the Sampler back.

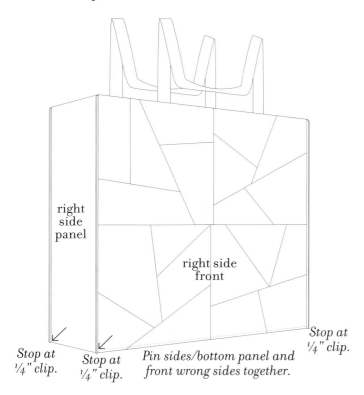

right side panel

right side front

Stop at ¼" clip.   Stop at ¼" clip.   Pin sides/bottom panel and front wrong sides together.   Stop at ¼" clip.

Button Closure

Fold the 1" x 12" strip in half lengthwise right sides together. Stitch. Turn right side out and press. Center the two ends of the strip on the top edge of the back. Baste in place.

button closure
12"
¼" x 12"

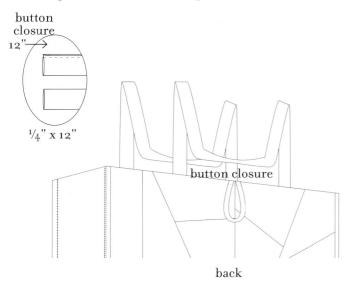

button closure

back

Binding

1. Piece the five binding strips together to form one continuous strip. Fold the binding in half lengthwise, wrong sides together, and press.

2. Using a ⅜" seam allowance bind the sides and bottom edges of the tote's front and back, treating the bottom corners as if you were binding the corners of a quilt.

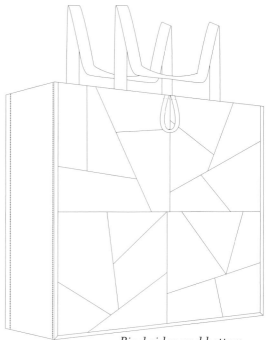

Bind sides and bottom.

Notes: Machine stitch the binding to the right side of the tote. Trim the top edges even with the top edge of the tote. Turn the binding and hand stitch to the Side/Bottom Panel.

When stitching the binding to the tote, you are sewing through several layers. Lengthen your stitch length and lighten the presser foot tension on your machine to make it easier to sew.

3. Place the handles inside the tote. Using a ⅜" seam allowance bind the top edge of the tote.

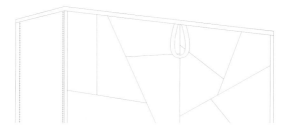

Note: Turn the four bound side edges toward the Sides/Bottom Panel when binding the top edge.

Be careful not to catch the handles in the top binding.

Finishing

1. Pull the handles up and out of the bag. Stitch the handles to the top edge of the Marquette Tote just below the binding. This will reinforce the handles.

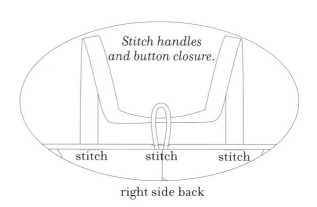

Stitch handles and button closure.

stitch   stitch   stitch

right side back

2. Press the Button Closure up. Stitch to the top edge of the binding.

3. Bring the Button Closure over the top of the tote and around the button. Depending on the size of the button, mark a line across the closure slightly above the button. Stitch back and forth across the closure on the marked line pulling the two sides of the closure together.

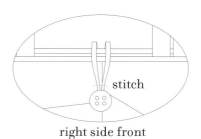

stitch

right side front

Optional Finishing Details:
Pull the Side/Bottom Panels out at the top edge. Fold in half. Sew two buttons together, one on either side of the panel. Repeat on both sides of the tote.

Fold the optional Lining sleeve in half lengthwise, right sides together, and stitch the bottom and side edges. Turn right side out and place foam core inside the sleeve. Place the covered foam core inside the bottom of the tote for a rigid bottom.

Scrappy Tidbits

Finished size: 18" x 18"

Scrappy Tidbits

Needle Artist: Janice Vaine, Jacksonville FL

This miniature quilt was a last minute addition to the book and is sure to become a much loved project. Easy piecing and a small surface to embroider makes this a good beginner project. It is a mini replica of the A Quilt to Dream Under quilt. Scrappy Tidbits is enchanting worked as a two-color quilt or totally scrappy.

FABRIC:

- Background—½ yard

- Patchwork Blocks—a variety of fat quarters or cotton fabric scraps

- Fan Blades—a variety of fat quarters or cotton fabric scraps

- Cotton Flannel—½ yard

- Backing—⅝ yard

- Binding—fat quarter

NOTIONS:

- 6-stranded embroidery floss in colors to complement fabrics

- 12 wt. Perle cotton in colors to complement fabrics

- Dear Jane® Tools by EZ Quilting

GENERAL INSTRUCTIONS:

Seam allowances are ¼" unless otherwise noted.
Press seams open.
Read through In the Classroom with Jan™ on pages 11-21 before beginning.

CUTTING AND MAKING THE PATCHWORK BLOCKS:

Note: You may choose to make eight of the same patchwork blocks or a variety of Blocks A, B, C, and D. Decide which blocks you wish to make before tracing and cutting the templates. I chose to use only patchwork Block A with curved template Block A3 in my Scrappy Tidbits Quilt.

- Reduce the Block A-D templates on pages 31-45 to 50%. If using the Curved Block templates on pages 46-47 reduce to 20%. Depending on the patchwork blocks you have chosen you may or may not need all the templates.

- Cut out templates 1-5 for Block A, B, C, and D using a variety of fat quarters or cotton fabric scraps. Cut fabric from the templates to make a total of eight blocks. See In the Classroom with Jan™ page 12 for cutting instructions and tips.

Make 8

1. Make eight patchwork blocks following the instructions on pages 14-20.

2. Trim the patchwork blocks to 5" square.

CUTTING AND MAKING THE FAN BLOCKS:

- 8— 6" squares from background

- 56 fan blades from fat quarters or scraps. Cut the blades using the Fan Favorite Blade Template on page 89. Refer to Tips for Cutting Blades on pages 89-90 and Color Option on page 87.

- Center circle using the template on page 87.

Note: Four of the eight fan blocks will form the center circle. It is important that the top edges of the fans are all $1\frac{1}{4}$" from the corner edges of the 6" background squares. This will ensure the circle matches at the seams and is round when pieced together.

1. Make eight Fan blocks following the instructions on pages 90-91. Appliqué the top edge only on four of the fans. These blocks will form the center circle and the raw edges will be covered with an appliquéd circle. Appliqué the top and bottom edges on the remaining four blocks.

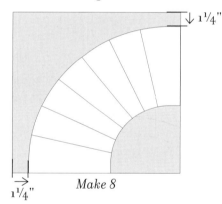

↓ $1\frac{1}{4}$"

→ $1\frac{1}{4}$"

Make 8

2. Trim the fan blocks to 5" square using the outside straight edges of the fans as an alignment guide.

Flannel:
- 20" square

Backing:
- 20" square

Single-Fold Binding:
- 4—$1\frac{1}{8}$" x 22" fabric strips

PUTTING IT ALL TOGETHER:

1. Lay out the six patchwork blocks and eight fan blocks in four rows with four blocks in each row, as shown. The four center fan blocks will create a Dresden plate.

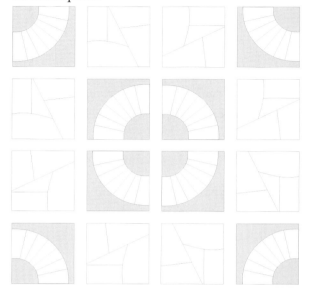

2. Sew the blocks together in rows. Sew the rows together to make the quilt top.

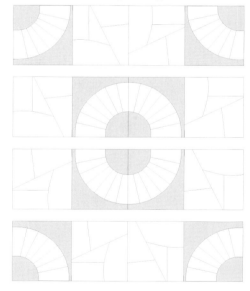

3. Center and appliqué the center circle in the middle of the Dresden plate.

4. Place the quilt top on the 20" flannel square. Baste the top and flannel together from the center out, vertically, horizontally, and diagonally.

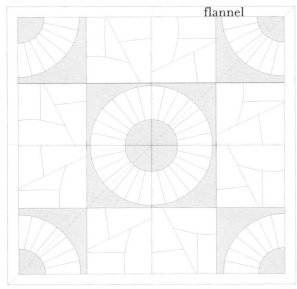

flannel

Baste top and flannel together.

5. Embroider the top edges of the fans and the seam lines of the patchwork block with stitches from pages 50-73 and stitch combinations from pages 130-133. Embroider motifs (pages 134-143) throughout the quilt as desired.

6. Place the embroidered quilt top on the wrong side of the backing. Tack the top and backing together, hiding the stitches at intersecting seam lines.

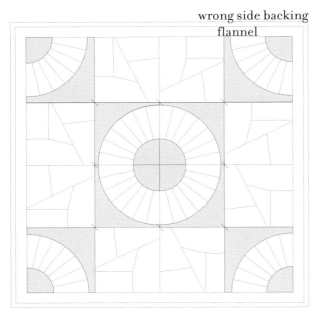

wrong side backing
flannel

7. Trim the quilt and flannel to 18½" square. Bind the quilt with single-fold binding.

8. Label the quilt, including your name, date, and place.

Scrappy Tidbits Color and Stitch Option
Needle Artist: Jo Ann Cridge, Annapolis, MD

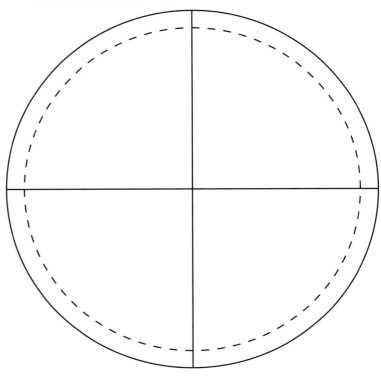

Center Circle Template
³⁄₁₆" seam allowances are included.

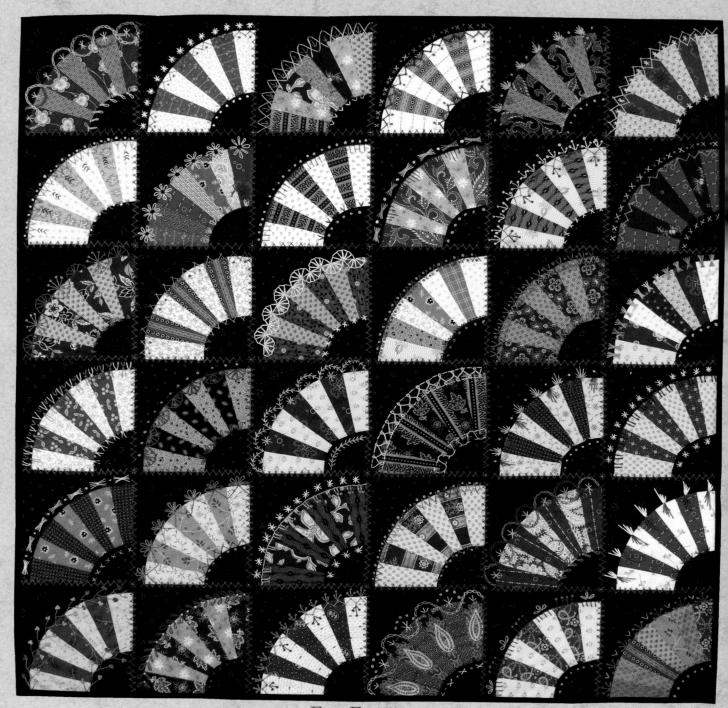

Fan Favorite

Finished size: 28" x 28"

Fan Favorite

Needle Artist: Natalie Tomola, Jacksonville, FL
Patchwork & Appliqué: Jo Ann Cridge, Annapolis, MD and Janice Vaine, Jacksonville, FL

This quilt was inspired by a delightful antique quilt dated 1897 by "M.B." Who was M.B.? And what does the number 75 stitched in the same block with the year and initials represent?

Everyone who sees this quilt falls in love. Each block becomes a mini quilt of its own and the stitching process becomes more addictive with each one. This quilt was made using Jo Morton fabrics by Amdover Fabrics. Thank you Jo for helping to make the replica a spectacular reproduction and a fan favorite!

FABRIC:

- Background—1¼ yards
- Fan Blades—fat quarters of lights, mediums, and darks
- Binding—¼ yard
- Backing—1 yard
- Muslin—1⅝ yards

CUTTING INSTRUCTIONS:

Background:

- 36—6" squares

FAN BLADES:

Each fan requires seven blades. Cut blades for 36 fans as follows:

- 18 fans have 4 lights and 3 medium/darks.
- 18 fans have 4 medium/darks and 3 lights.

TIPS FOR CUTTING BLADES:

1. Trace and cut out the Fan Favorite Blade Template leaving ⅛" of paper around the outside edge of the template. Place double-stick tape on the back of the paper template. Place the template on the right side of the fabric tape side down.

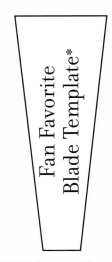

Fan Favorite
Blade Template*

*Add ¼" seam allowance.

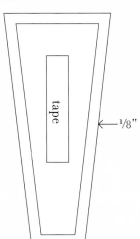

tape

← ⅛"

2. Use a ruler with ¼" markings to cut out the fabric blades adding the ¼" seam allowance to the outside edge. Replace the double-stick tape as needed.

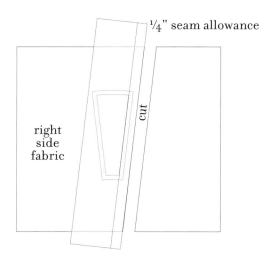

Option: Trace the template onto template plastic. Use as above to fussy cut blades to make unique fans.

Muslin:
- 36—7" squares

Backing:
- 27½" square
  (or finished size of quilt top plus ½")

Single-fold Binding:
- 4—1⅛" x width of fabric strips

Notions:
- 6-stranded embroidery floss in colors to complement fan blocks
- 12 wt. Perle cotton in colors to complement fan blocks
- Dear Jane® Tools by EZ Quilting®

GENERAL INSTRUCTIONS:
Seam allowances are ¼" unless otherwise noted. Press seams open.

Read through In the Classroom with Jan™, Embroidering the Sampler Blocks, on pages 22-27 before beginning.

MAKING THE FAN BLOCKS:

1. Sew seven blades together alternating lights and medium/darks. Make 36 fans—18 with light outside blades and 18 with medium/dark outside blades.

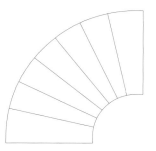

2. Mark a 5" square on the WRONG SIDE of each background square.

Tip: The 5" square in the Dear Jane® Tools by EZ Quilting® is ideal for marking and trimming the fan blocks for this quilt.

3. Place a pieced fan, right side down, on the wrong side of a background square. Align the side edges of the fan with the side edges of the 5" square. Pin. Machine baste the fan to the background with a ¼" seam allowance along the upper and lower curved edges of the fan.

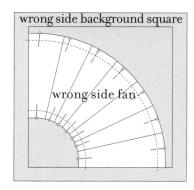

4. On the right side of the background square, mark along the inside edge right next to the basting stitches. CAREFULLY trim ONLY the background fabric $^{3}/_{16}$" from the marked line revealing the fan underneath.

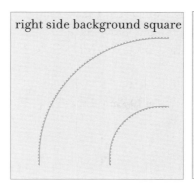 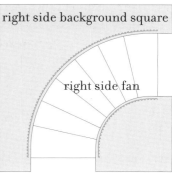

right side background square right side background square

right side fan

5. Starting on the top curve, remove a $^{1}/_{2}$" of the basting stitches. Use your needle to turn under the traced line and appliqué in place. Continue removing a $^{1}/_{2}$" of basting stitches, turning under the seam allowance and stitching along the curve. In the same manner, stitch the bottom curve. Repeat with the remaining fans and background squares. Make a total of 36 fan blocks.

 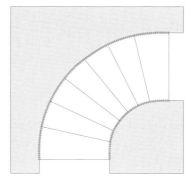

6. Mark a 5" square on the right side of the 36 fan blocks. Place a fan block on top of a 7" muslin square. Baste $^{1}/_{4}$" inside the traced 5" square. This will be your guide for adding embroidery.

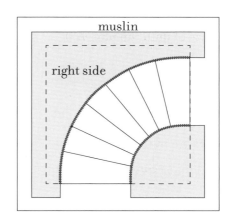

muslin

right side

7. Embroider the two curvededges of each fan with stitches from pages 50-73 and stitch combinations from pages 130-133.

8. Trim the blocks to 5" square using the outside straight edges of the fans as an alignment guide.

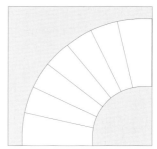

Trim to 5" square

PUTTING IT ALL TOGETHER:

1. Lay out the 36 fan blocks in six rows with six blocks in each row. Sew the blocks together in rows. Sew the rows together to make the quilt top.

Take note of the diagonal rows of lights and darks on the antique (page 93) and the reproduction (page 88) quilts .

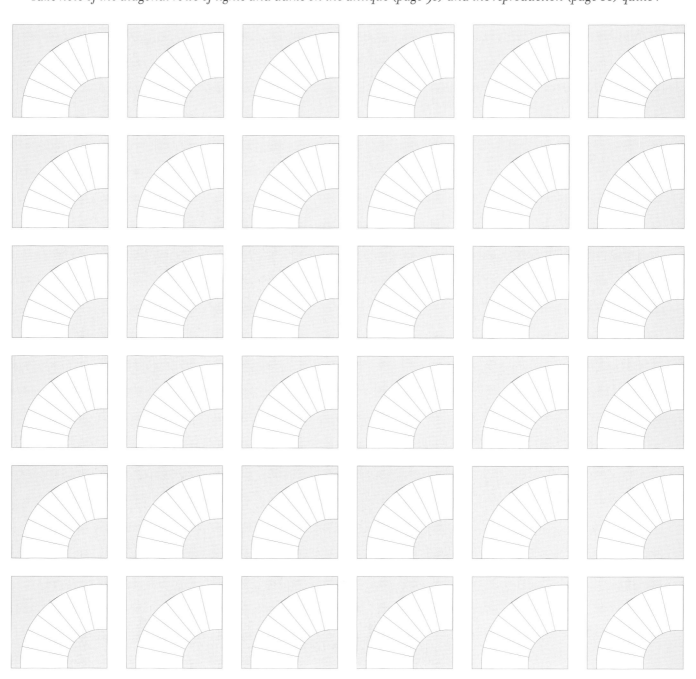

2. Embroider the vertical and horizontal joining seams with the Herringbone Stitch (page 65).

3. Layer the quilt top and backing wrong sides together. Pin. Baste along the outside edges. Make a small tacking stitch in the seam intersections joining the top and backing together.

4. Square up the quilt and trim. Bind the quilt with single-fold binding.

5. Label the quilt, including your name, date, and place.

Antique Fan Quilt in the collection of Janice Vaine

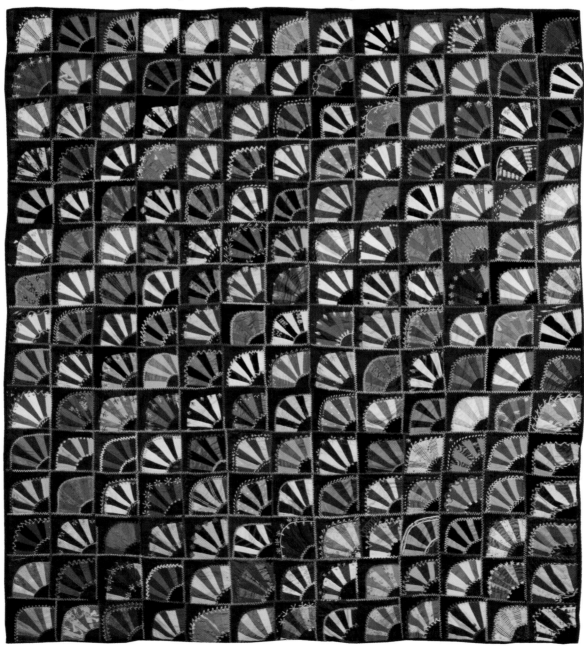

A Quilt to Dream Under

Finished size: 70" x 70"

A Quilt to Dream Under

Needle Artists: Annette Flockhart Brindle, Jacksonville, FL; Jo Ann Cridge, Annapolis, MD; Luella Dusek, Pittsburgh, PA; Kara Mason, Woodbine, MD; Janice Vaine, Jacksonville, FL; Teri A. Young, Monrovia, MD

This is a scrap-happy quilt. The patchwork is an opportunity to use up fabric leftovers, bits and pieces. It also gives you a chance to highlight those favorite fabric pieces you have collected over the years. The same is true for the threads you choose to complement the patchwork.

FABRIC:
Note: The Center Block is a striking quilt top on its own. These supplies are listed separately should you choose to only make the 36" x 36" Center Block.

Center Block:

- Dresden Plate Blades—assorted pieces of cotton, linen, silk, wool and/or velvet OR a Jelly Roll™

- Center Circle—fat quarter

- Background—1¼ yards

- Foundation—1⅝ yards cotton flannel

- Backing for Center Block only—1¼ yards

Patchwork Blocks and Corners:

- Dresden Plate Blades for Corner Blocks— assorted pieces of cotton, linen, silk, wool and/or velvet OR Jelly Rolls *(Note: One 40-piece Jelly Roll will make three blades per strip or a total of 120 blades. You need a total of 136 blades for the Center and Corner Blocks.)*

- Patchwork—assorted pieces of cotton, linen, silk, wool and/or velvet OR four Layer Cakes™ *(Note: If using Layer Cakes for piecing the Corners, some fabric will need to be pieced together for CP4 Template)*

- Corner Blocks—1 yard muslin

- Quarter Circles—fat quarter

- Foundation—3½ yards cotton flannel

- Backing for entire quilt—4½ yards

THREADS, NEEDLES FOR EMBROIDERY, AND NOTIONS:
See In the Classroom with Jan™, pages 8-10

- Bamboo Point Turner

- Threads used in this quilt may be found on page 96.

GENERAL INSTRUCTIONS:
Seam allowances are ¼" unless otherwise noted.

Press seams open unless otherwise noted. When sewing a lightweight and heavyweight fabric together, press the seam toward the lightweight fabric.

Be careful to press using an iron setting for the fabric being pressed. For instance, do not use a cotton setting to press silk or wool as it may burn the fabric. Consider using a small wooden press for delicate fabrics.

The embroidery on the quilt was done with two strands of 6-stranded embroidery floss or 1 strand of wool.

Methods for transfering design motifs for embroidery are found on pages 26-27.

When basting is indicated, machine baste using your sewing machine's even feed walking foot and longest basting stitch setting on your machine.

Note: I recommend hand-basting batiks. Machine basting can leave needle holes in batik fabrics.

Remove basting stitches as they intersect with embroidery stitches.

THREADS

Note: I have listed the threads used only as a guideline or if you wish to use the same threads and colors. Keep in mind each needle artist stitches with a different tension so your thread requirements may be more or less than those listed.

CENTER BLOCK:

The Gentle Art 5 yard skeins of 6-stranded embroidery floss:

- Sea Spray—5 skeins
- Presidential Blue—3 skeins
- Tropical Ocean—4 skeins
- Flax—6 skeins

The Gentle Art 10 yard skeins of wool:

- Buckeye Scarlet—9 skeins
- Oatmeal—8 skeins
- Ohio Lemon Pie—2 skeins
- Faded Rose—2 skein

PATCHWORK AND CORNER BLOCKS:

The Gentle Art 5 yard skeins of 6-stranded embroidery floss:

- Oatmeal—6 skeins
- Sea Spray—2 skeins
- Melon Patch—6 skeins
- Buckeye Scarlet—3 skeins
- Ohio Lemon—2 skeins
- Blue Jay—6 skeins
- Presidential Blue—3 skeins
- Peacock—4 skeins
- Tropical Ocean—6 skeins
- Flax—9 skeins
- Faded Rose—4 skeins

The Gentle Art 10 yard skeins of wool:

- Buckeye Scarlet—14 skeins
- Oatmeal—8 skeins
- Ohio Lemon Pie—7 skeins
- Faded Rose—4 skeins

CUTTING AND MAKING THE PATCHWORK BLOCKS:

Note: If making only the Center Block, skip this step and refer to Cutting and Making the Center Block.

Referring to the Cutting Instructions from In the Classroom with Jan™ on page 12 and using the block templates on pages 31-47, cut out enough fabric pieces to make eight 18" finished Sampler Blocks.

Note: You will need eight A blocks, eight B blocks, eight C blocks and eight D blocks. These patchwork blocks will then be sewn together in groups of four to make eight Sampler Blocks.

Following the instructions on pages 13-21, make eight Sampler Blocks.

CUTTING AND MAKING THE CENTER BLOCK:

- 64 blades using the Large Dresden Plate Blade Template on page 114.

Note: If using a combination of fabrics, you may need additional blades depending on the weight of the fabrics. The quilt shown used 68 blades, one additional blade for each quarter plate.

Background:

- Four 20" squares

Center Circle:

- One 14" square

Foundation:

- Four 20" squares
- One 15" square

Backing
if only making the Center Block:

- 36½" square

BLADE TRIMMING METHOD:

Trim the template, leaving an ⅛" of paper around the outside finished edge. Place several pieces of double-stick tape on the back of the template and place the template on the right side of the fabric tape side down. Use a rotary cutter and ruler to cut out the blade, adding a ¼" seam allowance from the finished edge of the blade template. Cut a total of 64 blades, replacing the double-stick tape as needed.

Note: The extra ⅛" of paper left on the outside edge of the template assures you will maintain an accurate template. Adding the ¼" seam allowance with the ruler and not on the paper template is more accurate. Over multiple cuts, slivers may be trimmed off of a ¼" paper seam allowance, changing the size of the template.

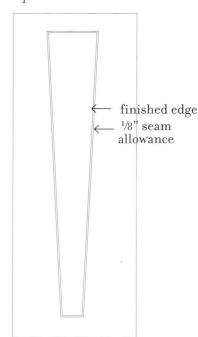

← finished edge
← ⅛" seam allowance

MAKING THE BLADES:

1. Fold the blade in half vertically, right sides together. Finger press the center of the blade, 4½" from the top edge.

2. Stitch along the top of the blade from cut edge to the fold. Backstitch two stitches at the fold to secure. More than two backstitches creates too much bulk and is difficult to turn.

3. Trim the seam allowance at an angle at the folded edge.

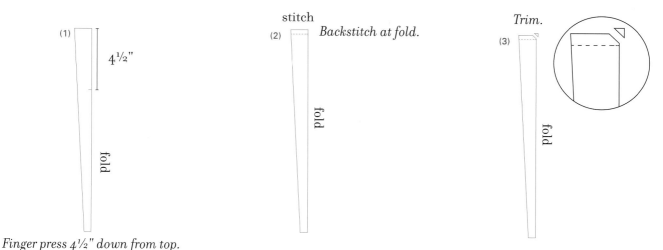

Finger press 4½" down from top.

4. Open the point matching the seam to the finger pressed fold line. This assures the point is centered on the blade. Using a Clover mini iron, press the seam only.

5. Turn the point right side out using a bamboo point turner. Align the seam with the finger pressed fold line. Press point. Make 64 blades.

Tip: Press delicate fabrics with a small wooden press.

6. Layer two blades, right sides together, matching points and side edges. Place the sewing machine needle ¼" down from top of seam. Backstitch to the edge and then continue sewing down the length of the blade. Press seam open.

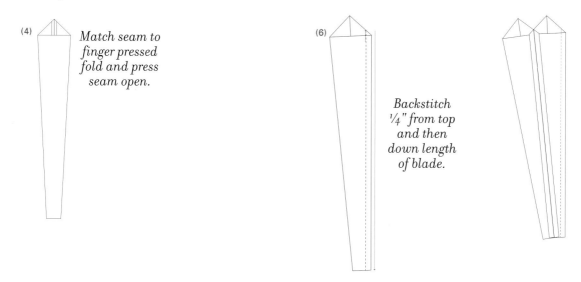

7. Sew another blade to the first two blades following steps 1-2.

8. Continue adding blades until there are 16 blades sewn together forming a quarter Dresden Plate. Make 4 quarter Dresden Plates.

Tip: Accuracy is important to forming a circle. There are a total of 64 blades in the full Dresden Plate. If you are off even a 1/16" on each seam, your plate will not lay flat.

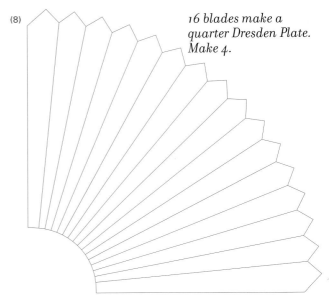

16 blades make a quarter Dresden Plate. Make 4.

MAKING THE DRESDEN PLATE:

1. Baste a 20" square of flannel and a 20" square of background fabric together horizontally, vertically, and diagonally, stitching from the center out to the edges. Baste around outside edges. Make four 20" background squares.

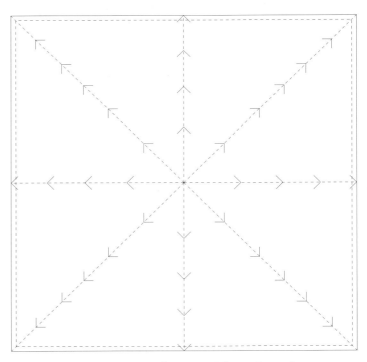

Baste background fabric and flannel together. Make 4.

2. On the right side of each background square, center and mark an 18½" square.

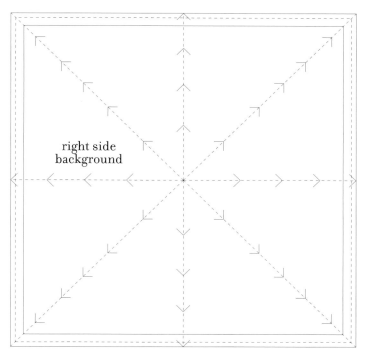

Mark an 18½" square.

3. Place one of the quarter Dresden Plates on the background fabric aligning the side edges of the quarter Dresden Plate with a right angle of the 18½" square. The top of the side edge of the two outside blades are 2" from the marked 18½" square. Pin in place. Baste the quarter Dresden Plate block as shown. Repeat on all four blocks.

Note: It is important to place the Dresden Plates in the same position on each background square. This will insure that the blades of the plate will match and form a round plate when the four blocks are sewn together.

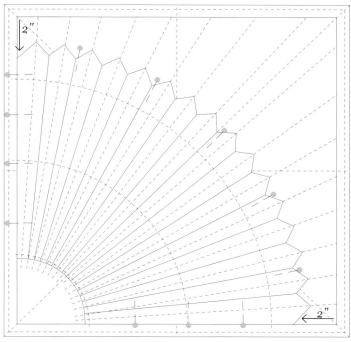

Pin and baste Dresden Plate to the background. Make 4.

4. Hand or machine appliqué the outer blades to the background. Make four quarter Dresden Plate blocks.

5. Referring to pages 26-27, mark two Corner Swag 1 and two Corner Swag 2 on the corners of the four blocks above the quarter Dresden Plate. Swag designs are on pages 135-136.

Note: Be mindful of the seam allowances. Keep motifs close to the plate so they will not be caught in the seam when the center block is pieced into the quilt.

6. Embroider the designs with a Backstitch (page 50) or a Stem Stitch (page 70).

Note: On A Quilt to Dream Under, the small bell shaped flowers on the Corner Swag 2 were stitched with multiple Straight Stitches (page 73). The flower calyxes were stitched with Colonial Knots (page 59) and one strand of floss.

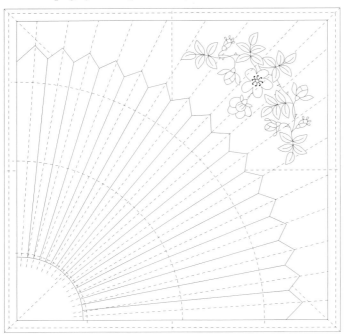

Corner Swag 1
Make 2.

Corner Swag 2
Make 2.

7. Using an 18½" square ruler, carefully trim ONLY the 90-degree right angles of each block as shown. Check to make sure the two outside blades on each block are equal distance from the marked 18½" square.

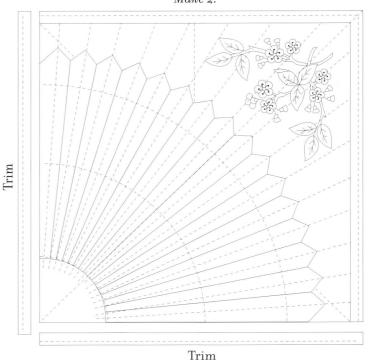

Trim

Trim

Trim sides of right angle.

8. Sew the four quarter Dresden Plate blocks together to form a Dresden Plate. Press seams open. The Dresden Plate should measure 34" point to point. The block is oversized and will be trimmed after the embroidery work is complete.

MAKING THE DRESDEN PLATE CENTER CIRCLE:

1. Finger press the horizontal and vertical centers of the 14" Center Circle square. Referring to pages 26-27, center and transfer the Center Rose Motif onto the block. Center and transfer the Small Leaf Wreath onto the block. Accurately transfer the 12" Outer Circle Template onto the block. Designs are on page 129.

2. Baste the marked block and the 15" flannel square together horizontally, vertically, and diagonally from the middle of the block out. Baste on the marked 12" outer circle.

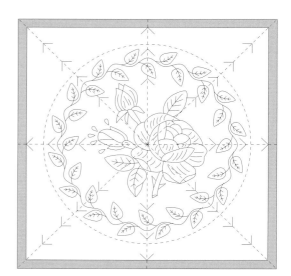

3. Embroider the Center Rose with a Stem Stitch (page 70). Using a lighter shade of thread, Stem Stitch on the inside edge of the previous stitches. Refer to the photo to see the double-stitched lines on the rose. Stem Stitch the leaves and the buds.

Note: The rose and buds were stitched with Buckeye Scarlet wool. The shading on the rose was stitched with Faded Rose wool. The stems, leaves and calyxes were stitched with Sea Spray.

4. Embroider the Small Leaf Wreath on the block. Use a Chain Stitch (page 56) for the vine and Stem Stitch (page 70) for the leaves. Remove the basting stitches where the basting line intersects with your embroidery stitches.

Note: The vine and leaves were both stitched with Ohio Lemon Pie.

5. Trim the FLANNEL FOUNDATION ONLY close to the 12" basted circle.

wrong side

Trim flannel foundation only.

6. On the right side, mark next to the outside edge of the 12" basted circle. Cut out the circle leaving a $^{3}/_{16}$" appliqué seam allowance.

7. Center the circle on the Dresden Plate, baste, and appliqué in place. Remove the basting stitches as you appliqué, turning the seam allowance under the flannel.

Color and Stitch Option
A Fan for All Seasons
Needle Artist:
Jo Ann Cridge
Annapolis, MD

DRESDEN PLATE EMBROIDERY:

1. Stitch nine rows of the Herringbone Stitch (page 65) around the outer edge of the appliquéd circle. The thread order used was: Oatmeal, Buckeye Scarlet, Flax, Presidential Blue, Oatmeal, Presidential Blue, Flax, Buckeye Scarlet, and Oatmeal.

2. On every other blade seam, mark a dot 2" from the edge of the 12" circle. Make a seven-stitch Straight Stitch Fan (page 73) with the center stitch going from the edge of the Herringbone Stitches to the marked dot. The inside fans were stitched with Oatmeal, Sea Spray, Buckeye Scarlet, Flax, Presidential Blue, Oatmeal, Sea Spray, and Buckeye Scarlet.

3. Starting at the tips of the blades and working toward the center, stitch five rows of Chain Stitches (page 56). The thread order was: Oatmeal, Buckeye Scarlet, Flax, Presidential Blue, and Oatmeal.

4. On every blade seam, mark a dot 2½" from the valley of the fan blades. Make a seven-stitch Straight Stitch Fan (page 73) with the center stitch going from the last row of the Chain Stitches to the marked dot. The outer fans were stitched with Oatmeal, Sea Spray, Buckeye Scarlet, Flax, and Presidential Blue.

5. Top each stitch on the outside fans with a Bullion Loop (page 53). The thread combinations on the outer fans were: Oatmeal topped with Buckeye Scarlet, Sea Spray topped with Oatmeal, Buckeye Scarlet topped with Oatmeal, Flax topped with Sea Spray, and Presidential Blue topped with Buckeye Scarlet.

6. Mark the outer edge of the Maple Leaf Vine Template (page 128) on the Dresden Plate between the embroidered fans. Align the bottom concave curved edge of the template with the outer edge of the appliquéd circle. Mark the template along the convex curve eight times. Embroider the vine with Chain Stitches (page 56).

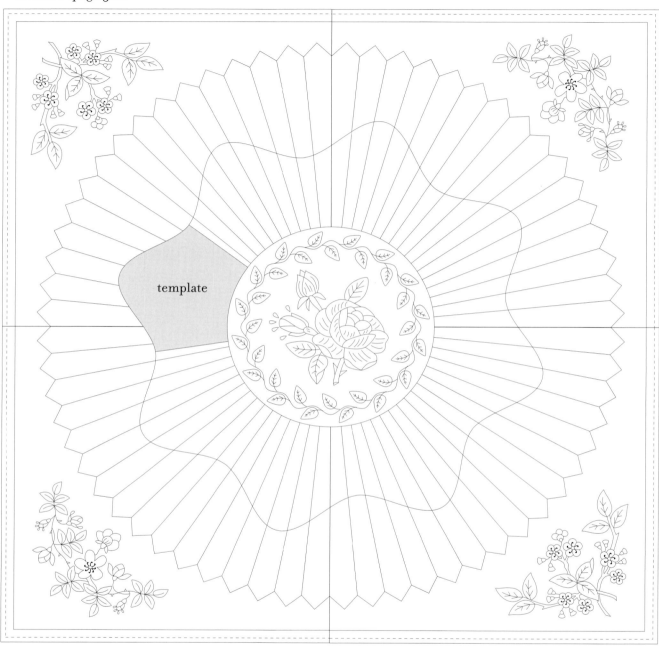

7. Referring to pages 26-27, transfer a Maple Leaf in each valley of the vine. There are a total of 16 Maple Leaves. There are two mirror-imaged leaves. Note the placement of the leaves on the vine. The Maple Leaf templates are on page 141.

8. Embroider the leaves and the leaf veins with a Stem Stitch (page 70). Add Fly Stitches (page 64) to the veins as desired.

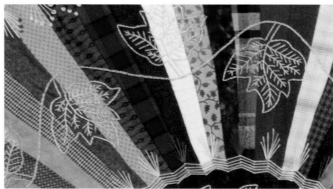

9. Square up and mark the block to 36½" square. It is best to mark the block and check that it is square before trimming. Trim the block to 36½" square.

Trim to 36½" square

FINISHING CENTER BLOCK ONLY:

Note: If you are making the full quilt, skip this step and continue with Cutting and Making the Corner Blocks.

1. Place the block and backing right sides together. Pin. Stitch the block and backing together leaving a 12" opening for turning.

2. Turn the block right side out. Stitch the opening closed. Carefully press the outside edges rolling the backing to the back.

3. Carefully hand baste the block and backing together vertically, horizontally, diagonally and around the outside edge. Quilt around the Center Rose, leaves and buds, the vine of the Small Leaf Wreath, the vine of the Maple Leaf Wreath, and the outer points of the Dresden Plate.

4. Place a label on the back of the block with your name, date, and location.

CUTTING AND MAKING THE CORNER BLOCKS:

Note: The Corner Block Template CP9 is cut from muslin.

Following the Cutting Instructions for the Center Block on page 96, cut 64 blades for the four corner Dresden plates

- From the flannel cut four 20" squares
- Cut 4 quarter circles using the Corner Quarter Circle template on page 140.

1. Make four quarter Dresden Plates following the instructions for Making the Blades on page 97 and Making the Dresden Plate, steps 1-7, on pages 98-100.

2. Using the fabric remaining from the Patchwork Blocks and the Pieced Corner Templates on pages 115-127, cut out four Corner Blocks. Remember, Corner Block template CP9 is cut from muslin.

3. Referring to the Block Map and the arrows on the diagrams, sew the corner block pieces right sides together. Press seams after each piece is added.

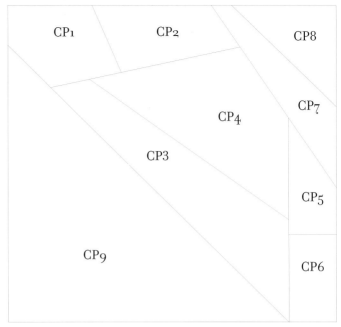

Block Map

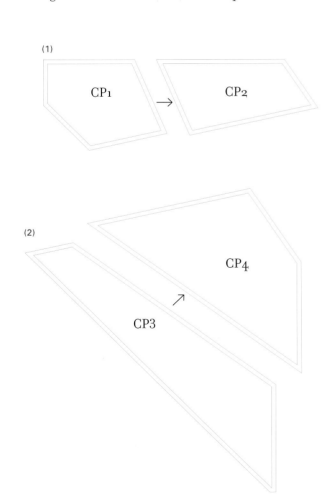

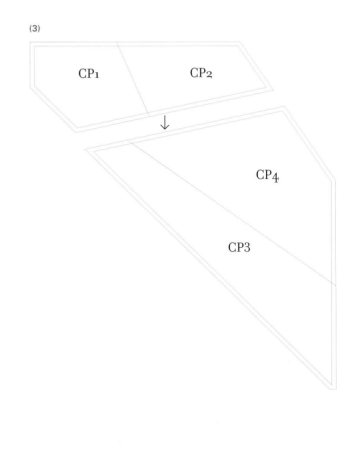

(4)

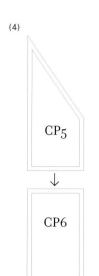

CP5

↓

CP6

(5)

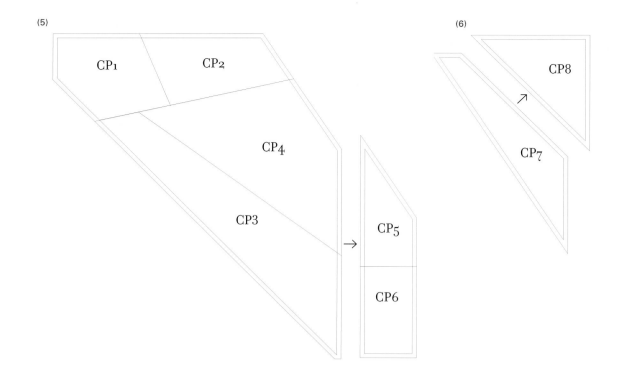

CP1 CP2

CP4

CP3

→ CP5

CP6

(6)

CP8

↗

CP7

(7) *Make four Corner Blocks.*

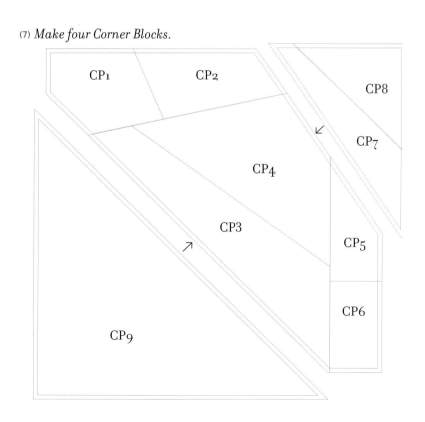

CP1 CP2

CP8

↙ CP7

CP4

CP3 CP5

↗

CP6

CP9

4. Baste a Corner Block and a 20" flannel square together horizontally, vertically, and diagonally stitching from the center out to the edges. Baste around the outside edge. On the right side of the Corner Block, center and mark an 18½" square. Make four.

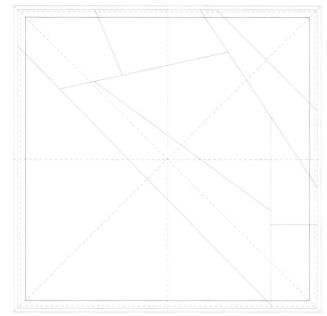

Baste. Center and mark an 18½" square on the block. Make four.

5. Place one of the quarter Dresden Plates on a Corner Block aligning the side edges of the quarter Dresden Plate with a right angle of the 18½" square. Pin in place. Baste the quarter Dresden Plate block as shown.

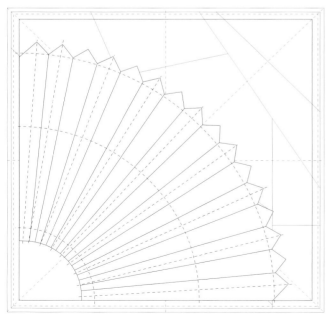

Pin and baste the quarter Dresden Plate to the Corner Block.

6. Hand or machine appliqué the Corner Quarter Circle on the bottom of the quarter Dresden Plate. Baste the side edges of the quarter circle in place. Repeat on each Corner Block.

Note: The side edges of the quarter circle align to the 90-degree angle of the marked 18½" square.

7. Hand or machine appliqué the outside edges of the blades to the background on all four Corner Blocks.

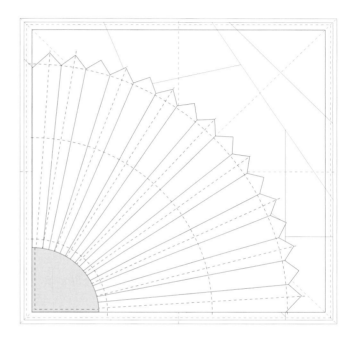

8. Referring to pages 26-27, transfer Corner Swags 3-5 (pages 137-139) onto the quarter Dresden Plates. Use one motif twice. Embroider the designs with a Stem Stitch (page 70).

Corner Block

9. Embroider the Corner Block patchwork seams with desired stitches and stitch combinations. Embroider a motif in the Corner Block Quarter Circles of each block. Embroider stitch combinations at the tops of the blades and along the curved edge of the quarter circle.

Note: Annette Flockhart Brindle embroidered the four Corner Patchwork blocks of the quilt. She stitched an additional motif over the corner patchwork and then embroidered the seams. She chose a quarter of the Small Leaf Wreath to embroider in the Corner Block Quarter Circle.

PUTTING IT ALL TOGETHER:

1. Trim each of the four Corner Blocks and eight Sampler Blocks to 18½" square.

2. Assemble the quilt in rows as shown. Sew the rows together.

3. Finish the quilt following the instructions for Finishing Center Block Only (page 108).

Option: Place the front and backing wrong sides together. Tack or quilt the top and backing together. Bind.

Tip: The original antique quilt was hand quilted, stitching in the ditch of the seams of the patchwork. You could also tie the quilt top and backing together in the intersections of the seams.

4. Label the quilt, including your name, date, and place.

* ALL TEMPLATES AND MOTIFS ARE 100% UNLESS NOTED OTHERWISE.
ADD 1/4" SEAM ALLOWANCE.

Dresden Plate
Blade Template
* ENLARGE 110%

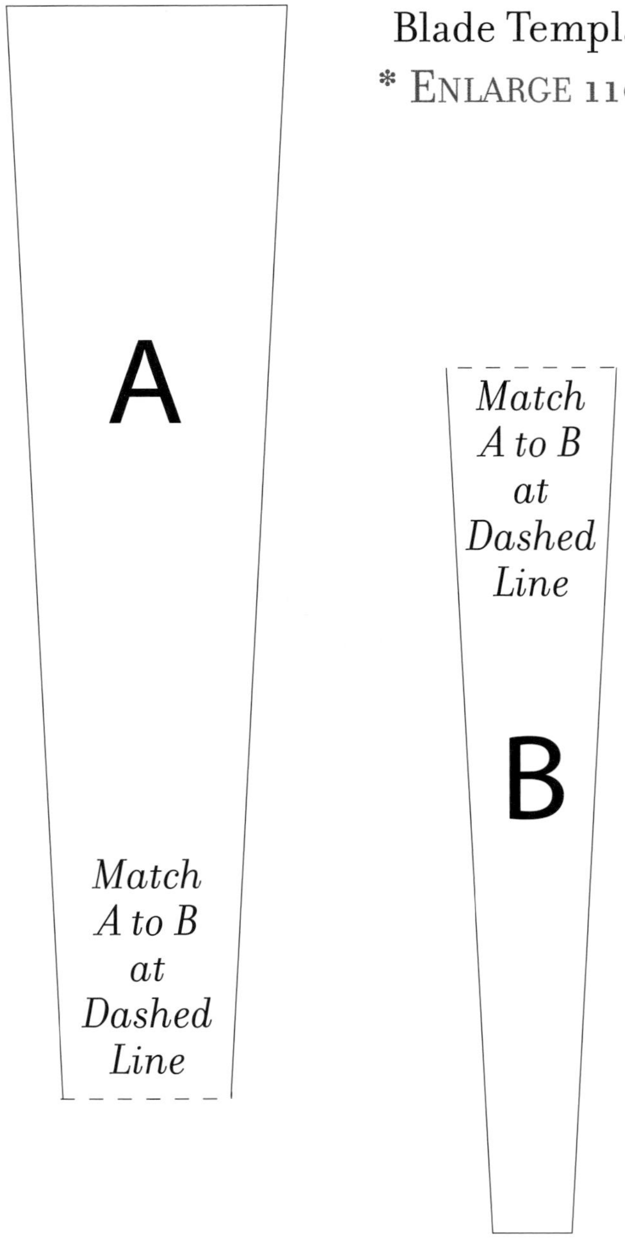
A
Match A to B at Dashed Line
Match A to B at Dashed Line
B

Pieced Corner
Template 1
* ENLARGE 110%

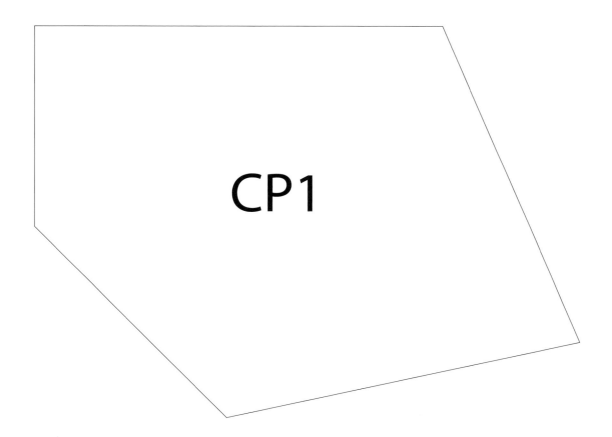

CP1

Pieced Corner
Template 3
* ENLARGE 110%

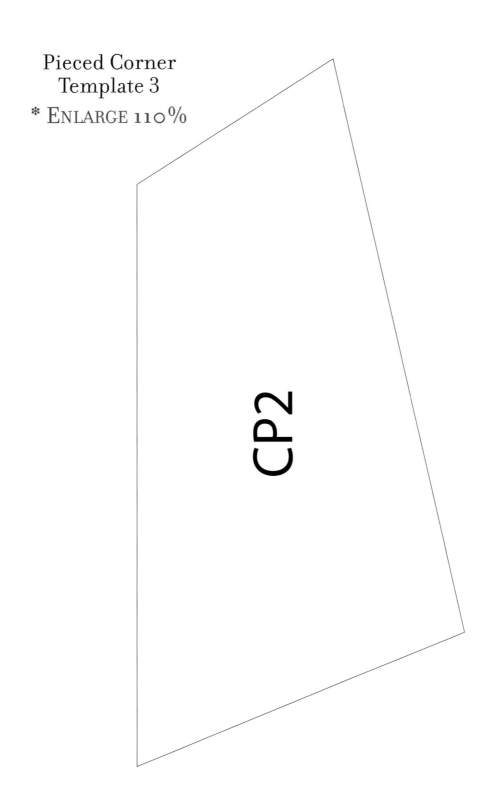

CP2

*ALL TEMPLATES AND MOTIFS ARE 100% UNLESS NOTED OTHERWISE. ADD ¼" SEAM ALLOWANCE.

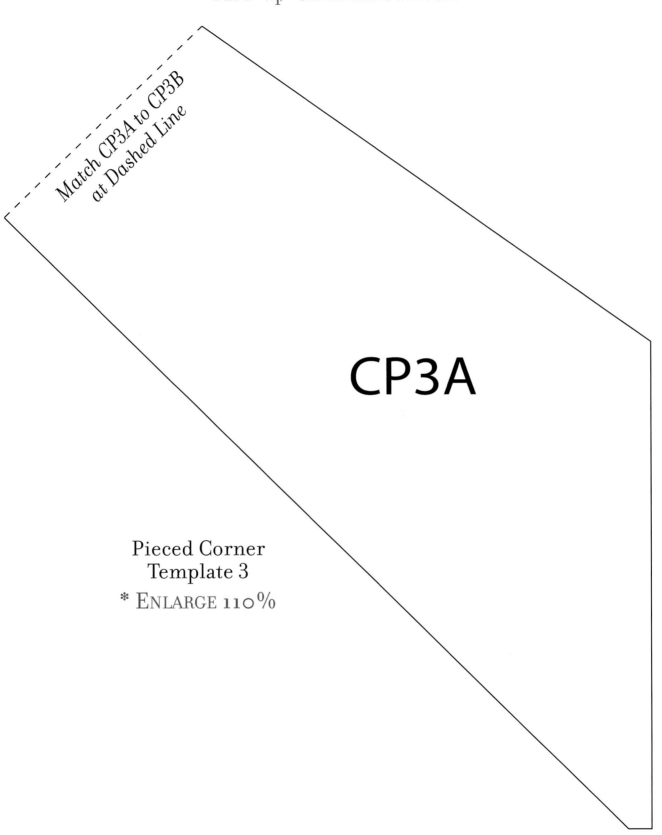

Match CP3A to CP3B at Dashed Line

CP3A

Pieced Corner
Template 3
* ENLARGE 110%

* ALL TEMPLATES AND MOTIFS ARE 100% UNLESS NOTED OTHERWISE.
ADD ¼" SEAM ALLOWANCE.

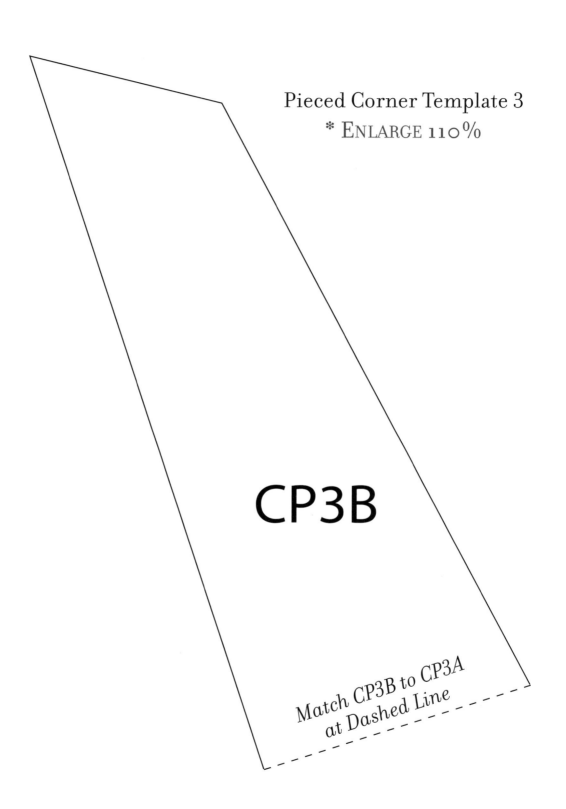

Pieced Corner Template 3
* ENLARGE 110%

CP3B

Match CP3B to CP3A
at Dashed Line

* ALL TEMPLATES AND MOTIFS ARE 100% UNLESS NOTED OTHERWISE.
ADD ¼" SEAM ALLOWANCE.

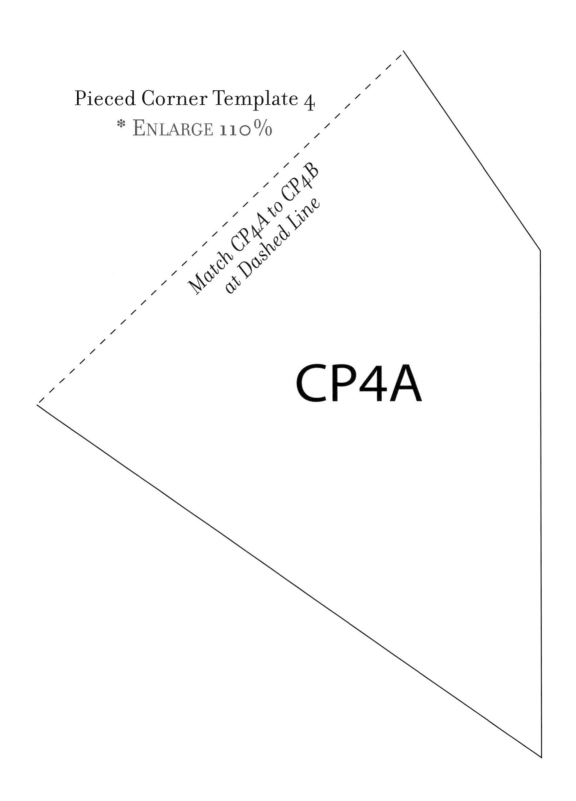

Pieced Corner Template 4
* ENLARGE 110%

Match CP4A to CP4B
at Dashed Line

CP4A

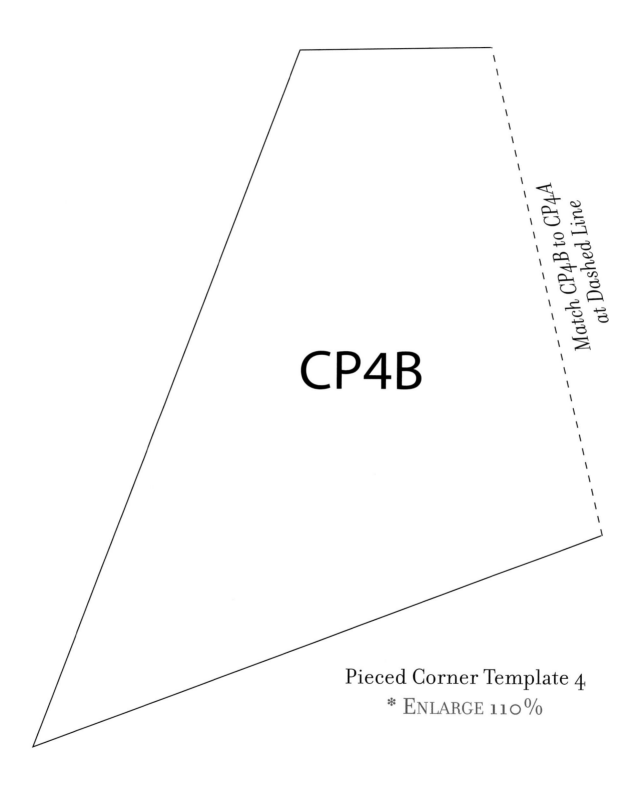

CP4B

Match CP4B to CP4A at Dashed Line

Pieced Corner Template 4
* ENLARGE 110%

* ALL TEMPLATES AND MOTIFS ARE 100% UNLESS NOTED OTHERWISE:
ADD ¼" SEAM ALLOWANCE.

Pieced Corner Template 5
* ENLARGE 110%

Pieced Corner Template 6
* ENLARGE 110%

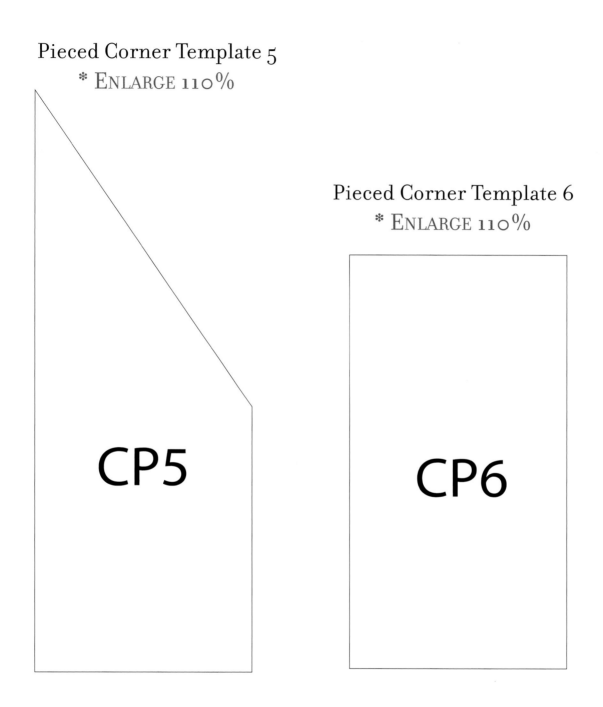

CP5

CP6

Pieced Corner Template 7
* ENLARGE 110%

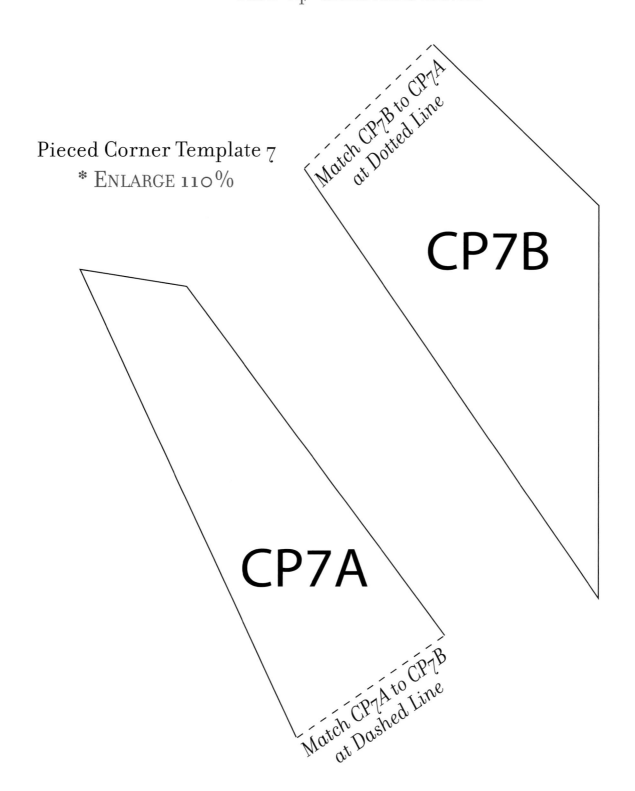

Match CP7B to CP7A
at Dotted Line

CP7B

CP7A

Match CP7A to CP7B
at Dashed Line

* ALL TEMPLATES AND MOTIFS ARE 100% UNLESS NOTED OTHERWISE.
ADD ¼" SEAM ALLOWANCE.

Pieced Corner Template 8
* ENLARGE 110%

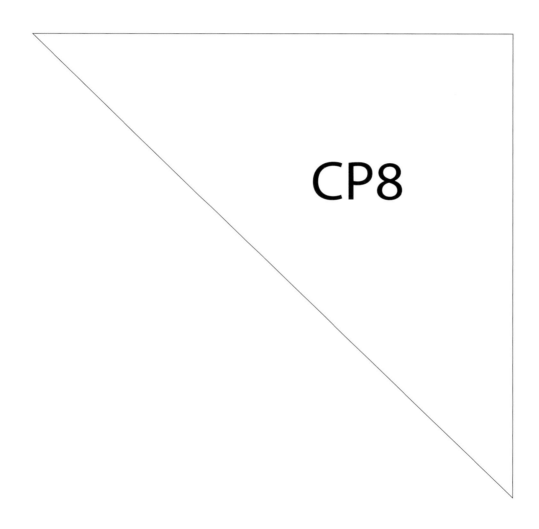

CP8

*ALL TEMPLATES AND MOTIFS ARE 100% UNLESS NOTED OTHERWISE. ADD ¼" SEAM ALLOWANCE.

Pieced Corner
Template 9
*ENLARGE 110%

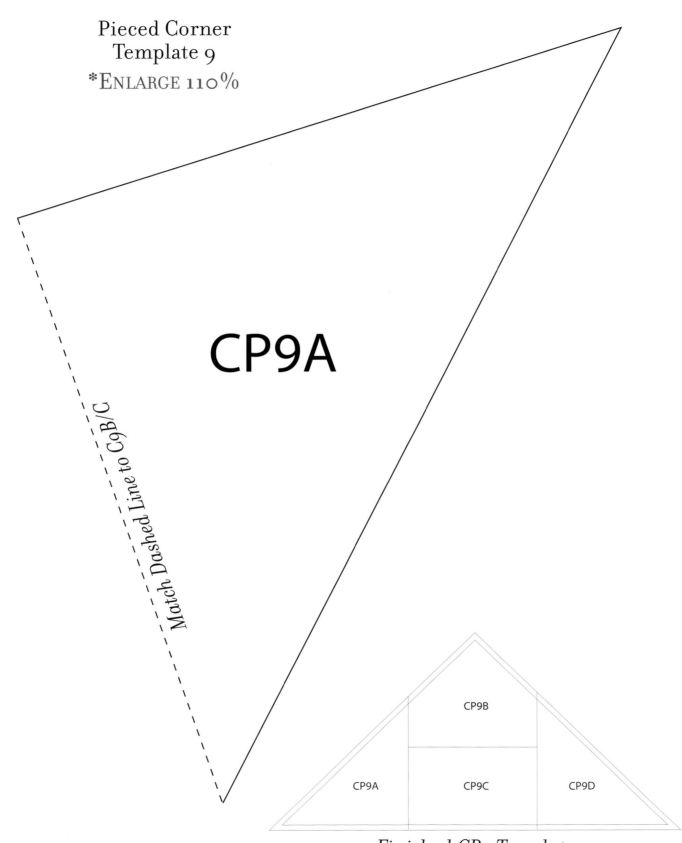

CP9A

Match Dashed Line to C9B/C

CP9B

CP9A   CP9C   CP9D

Finished CP9 Template

*ALL TEMPLATES AND MOTIFS ARE 100% UNLESS NOTED OTHERWISE.
ADD ¼" SEAM ALLOWANCE.

Pieced Corner
Template 9
*ENLARGE 110%

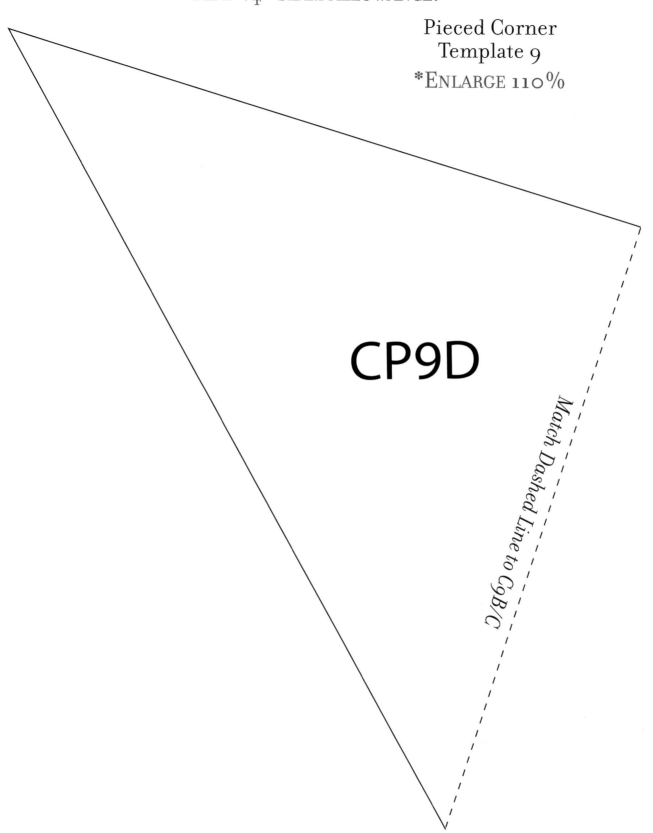

CP9D

Match Dashed Line to C9B/C

Pieced Corner
Template 9
*ENLARGE 110%

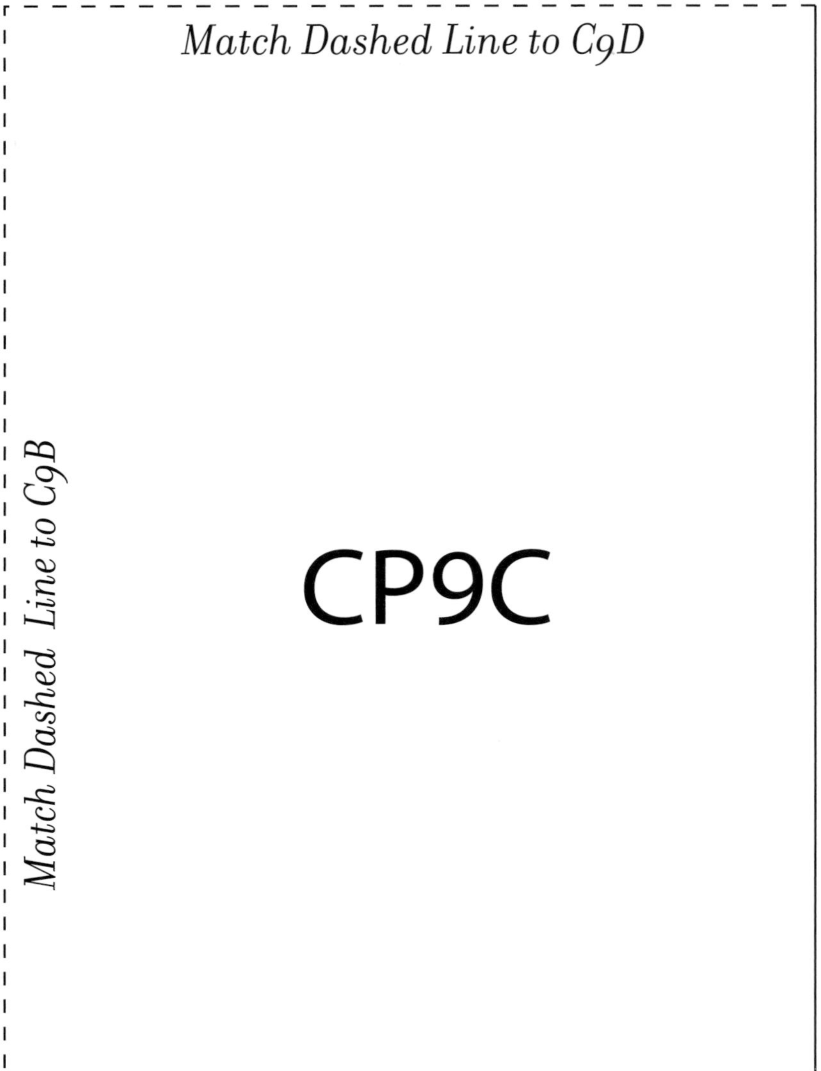

Match Dashed Line to C9D

Match Dashed Line to C9B

CP9C

Match Dashed Line to C9A

*ALL TEMPLATES AND MOTIFS ARE 100% UNLESS NOTED OTHERWISE.
ADD ¼" SEAM ALLOWANCE.

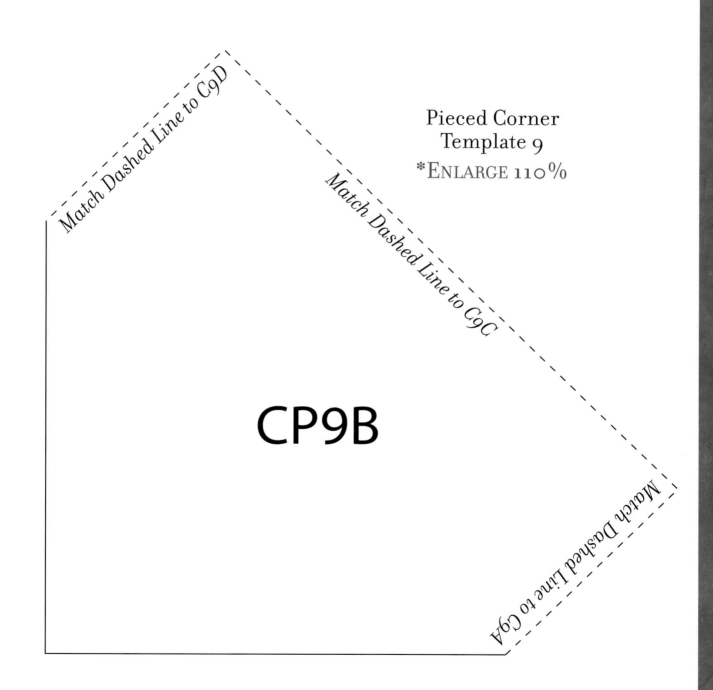

Match Dashed Line to C9D

Match Dashed Line to C9C

Pieced Corner
Template 9
*ENLARGE 110%

CP9B

Match Dashed Line to C9A

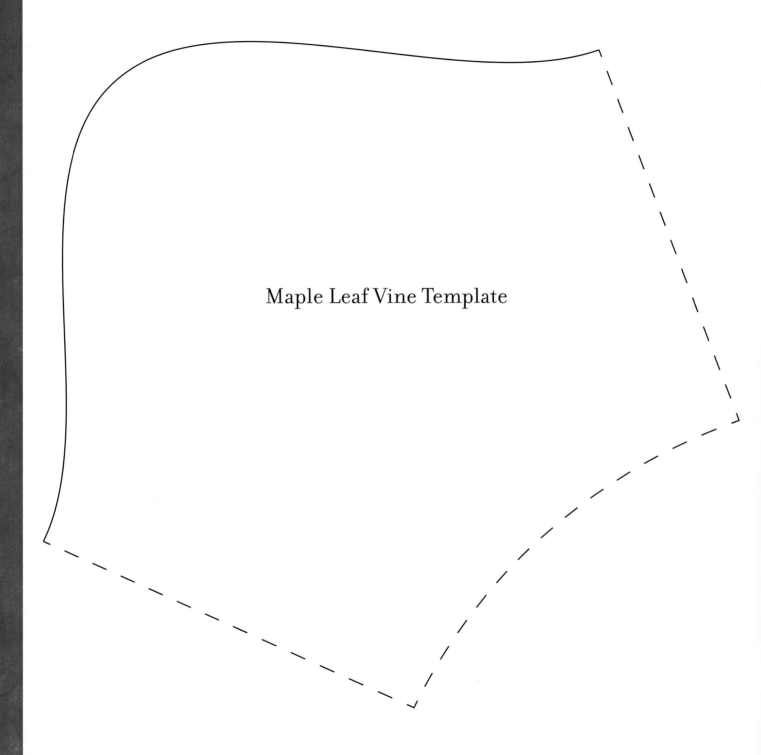

Maple Leaf Vine Template

* ALL TEMPLATES AND MOTIFS ARE 100% UNLESS NOTED OTHERWISE.
ADD 3/16" SEAM ALLOWANCE TO CURVED EDGE ONLY.

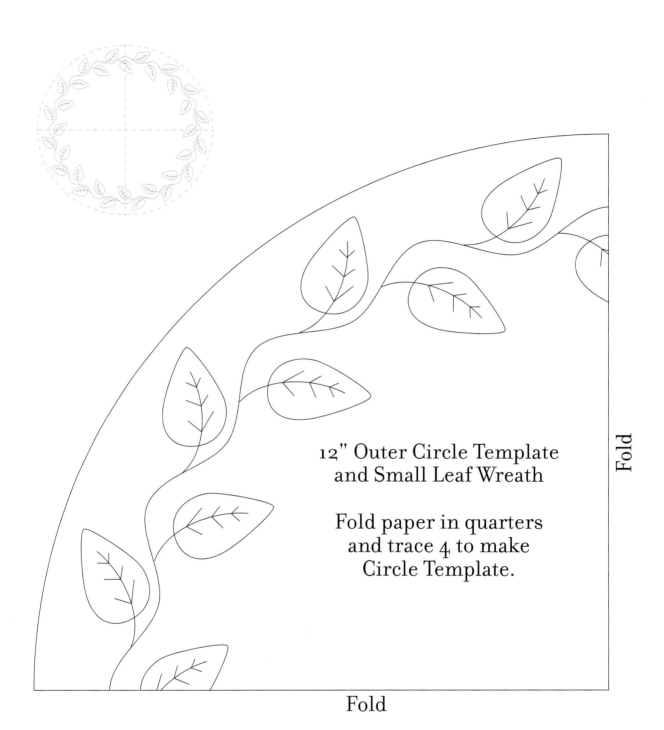

12" Outer Circle Template
and Small Leaf Wreath

Fold paper in quarters
and trace 4 to make
Circle Template.

Fold

Fold

Stitch Combinations

The following pages offer a small sampling of what can be accomplished with the 19 stitches on pages 50-73. The myriad of options for combining and varying these basic stitches is open to endless creative possibilities. I have listed a few suggestions for making stitch combinations. An example of stitches to experiment with is in parenthesis.

- stack individual stitches on top of each other (Fly Stitch)

- stitch two rows of the same stitch side by side, pointing the rows in the same direction or turning one row upside down (Buttonhole Stitch)

- add one stitch on the top and/or the bottom of a row of base stitches (base row of Backstitches with Lazy Daisy Flowers above and below)

- use curves and angles instead of straight lines of stitches and add another stitch in the valleys of the curves (stitch curves with the Stem Stitch and add Cross Stitch stars in the valleys of the curves)

- layer a row of stitches on top of a base row of stitches with a different color (Herringbone Stitch)

- scatter stitches on a solid fabric to give it texture (Colonial Knot or Cross Stitch)

Let your imagination and creativity paint a palette of stitches. There are no mistakes, only opportunities to practice and explore the wonderful world of embroidery.

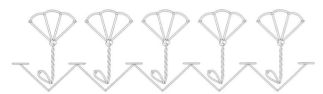

Blanket Stitch, Stem Stitch, Colonial Knot, Chain Stitch Detached, Straight Stitch

Fly Stitch, Colonial Knot, Chain Stitch Detached, Straight Stitch

Stem Stitch, Chain Stitch Detached, Colonial Knot

Buttonhole Stitch Up and Down, Straight Stitch, Colonial Knot

Blanket Stitch, Stem Stitch, Chain Stitch Detached

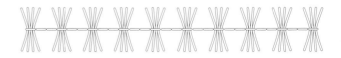

Sheaf Stitch, Backstitch

Bullion Stitch, Chain Stitch Detached,
Feather Stitch

Blanket Stitch, Colonial Knot

Blanket Stitch, Chain Stitch Detached, Herringbone
Stitch, Straight Stitch

Chain Stitch, Straight Stitch

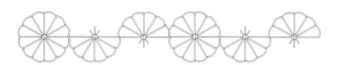

Chain Stitch, Straight Stitch, Chain Stitch Detached,
Colonial Knot

Herringbone Stitch, Colonial Knot

Blanket Stitch, Straight Stitch, Colonial Knot

Chain Stitch, Pistil Stitch

Chain Stitch Detached, Colonial Knot

Straight Stitch

Chain Stitch Detached, Colonial Knot

Herringbone Stitch, Colonial Knot, Cross Stitch

Chain Stitch, Fly Stitch, Straight Stitch,
Colonial Knot

Chain Stitch, Chain Stitch Detached, Straight
Stitch, Colonial Knot, Pistil Stitch, Fly Stitch

Herringbone Stitch, Chain Stitch Detached

Chain Stitch, Straight Stitch, Bullion Loops

Straight Stitch, Chain Stitch, Chain Stitch
Detached, Pistil Stitch, Colonial Knot

Laced Cretan Stitch, Chain Stitch Detached

Feather Stitch, Chain Stitch Detached

Chain Stitch, Chain Stitch Detached, Straight
Stitch, Colonial Knot

Herringbone Stitch, Straight Stitch, Colonial Knot

Chain Stitch, Straight Stitch

Fly Stitch

Straight Stitch, Lazy Daisy

Straight Stitch, Colonial Knot

Chain Stitch, Fly Stitch

Fly Stitch, Chain Stitch Detached, Colonial Knot

Chain Stitch, Chain Stitch Detached

Backstitch, Chain Stitch

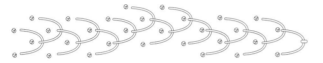

Feather Stitch, Colonial Knot

Fly Stitch, Colonial Knot

Chain Stitch, Blanket Stitch, Stem Stitch,
Chain Stitch Detached

Chain Stitch, Colonial Knot

Herringbone Stitch, Straight Stitch, Colonial Knot

Cross Stitch, Backstitch

Buttonhole Stitch Up and Down, Colonial Knot

Chain Stitch, Straight Stitch

Bullion Stitch, Chain Stitch Detached, Pistil Stitch

Buttonhole Stitch, Straight Stitch, Fly Stitch,
Chain Stitch Detached

Straight Stitch, Chain Stitch Detached

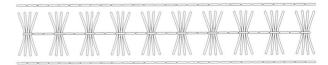

Sheaf Stitch, Backstitch

Chain Stitch, Chain Stitch Detached, Colonial Knot

133

Center Rose Motif

Corner Swag 1
* ENLARGE 130%

Corner Swag 2
* ENLARGE 130%

Corner Swag 3

* ENLARGE 130%

Corner Swag 4
* ENLARGE 130%

Corner Swag 5
* ENLARGE 130%

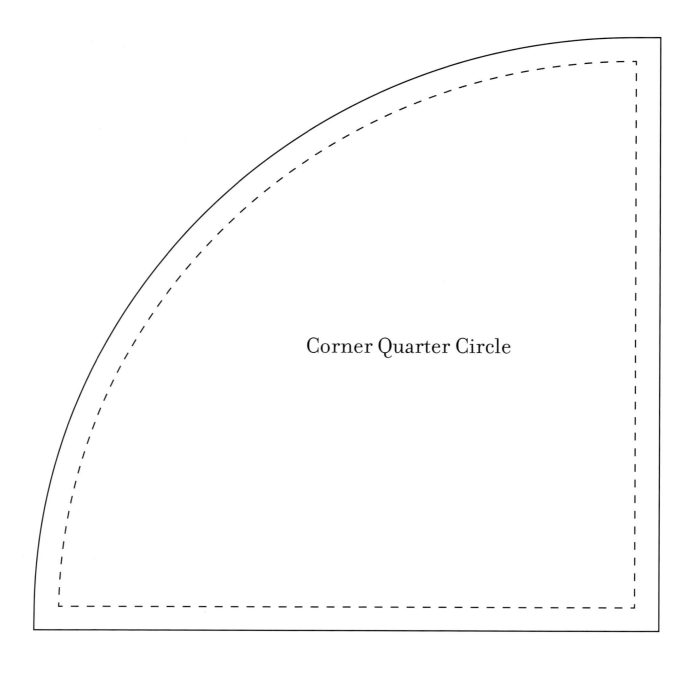

Corner Quarter Circle

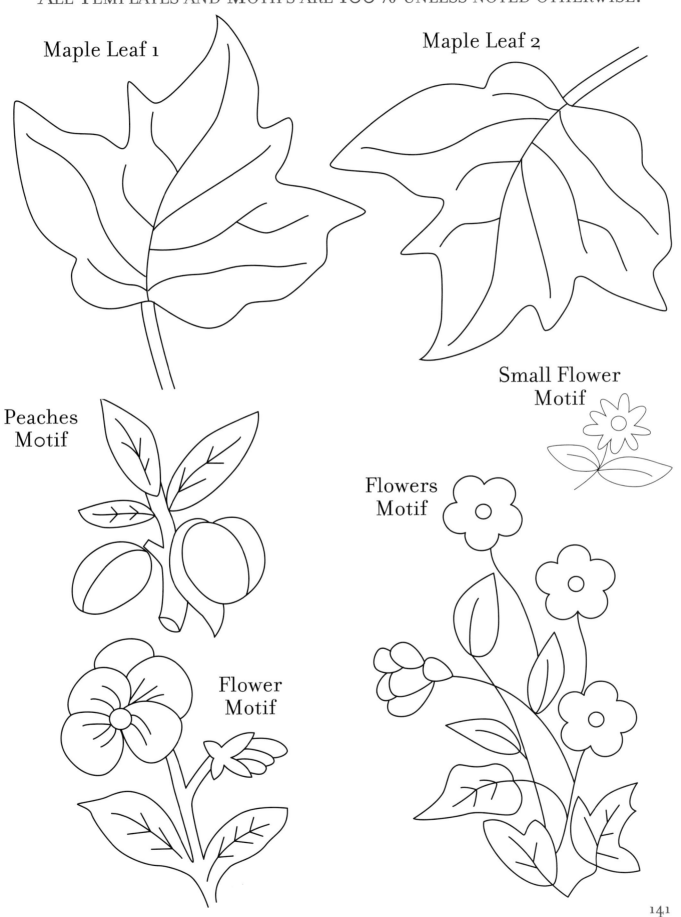

Maple Leaf 1

Maple Leaf 2

Peaches
Motif

Small Flower
Motif

Flowers
Motif

Flower
Motif

Flowers
Motif

Bird
Motif

Flower
Motif

Flower
Motif

Flower
Motif

Flower
Motif

Plant
Motif

Leaf
Motif

Leaf
Motif

Flower
Motif

Flower
Motif

Flower
Motif

Flower
Motif

Flower
Motif

Flower
Motif

Flower
Motif

Flower
Motif

About the Author

Jan is a hand appliqué, embroidery, and petite piecing enthusiast. Jan's mom taught her to sew at the age of 5 and her love of the needle has kept her in stitches ever since.

In 2004, Jan's passion for sewing and designing blossomed into her pattern company, The Graham Cracker Collection. She has authored five books since 2011.

Jan is inspired by vintage embroidery, antique quilts and the lessons she learns from the needle artists. Jan shares her learning experience by teaching for quilt guilds, quilt shops and conferences across the U.S. and Canada. She is a frequent instructor at The Elly Sienkiewicz Appliqué Academy and her local quilt shop in Jacksonville, Florida.

Jan is devoted to sharing the gentle art of handwork. She hopes appliqué and embroidery remain relevant and relatable to today's quilter and are enthusiastically embraced by future generations of needle artists.

www.grahamcrackercollection.com

Janice Vaine
Jacksonville, FL

Acknowledgements

A heartfelt thank you to the following needle artists for sharing their time and talent. You made this book a reality.

Annette Flockhart Brindle, Jo Ann Cridge, Doris Dowling, Luella Dusek, Elin Ely, Kara Mason, Brenda G. Moore, Joan Rawls, Helen Anne Roesler, Buffy Schenkel, Pat Veynar, Marjorie Hill Via, Ronda Geisler Woods, Teri A. Young

A special thank you to the following companies and individuals for the fabric and thread contributions that brought the quilts and projects to life.

Andover Fabrics, Jo Morton; The Gentle Art, Jim and Kristi Pfeifer; Moda Fabrics, Lissa Alexander; Threadnuts, Jane Garrison; Valdani, Inc., Dana Jonsson

And most importantly to my husband, Joe, for your faith in me, all your encouragement, support, guidance, and love. Thank you!

Resources

Andover Fabrics, Inc.
1384 Broadway, Suite 1500 New York, NY 10018
www.andoverfabrics.com

The Gentle Art
P.O. Box 670, New Albany, OH 43054
www.thegentleart.com

Landauer Publishing LLC
3100 101st Street, Urbandale, IA 50322
www.landauerpub.com

Morgan Hoops
8040 Erie Avenue, Chanhassen, MN 55217
www.nosliphoops.com

Schamber Quilts
1304 West Stirrup Way, Payson, AZ 85541
www.sharonschamber.com,
www.purpledaisiesllc.com

Threadnuts
912 Silver Charm Lane, York, SC 29745
threadnuts.com

Valdani, Inc.
3551 – 199 Street, Edmonton, AB, T6M 2N5, Canada
www.valdani.com

United Notions/Moda Fabrics
13800 Hutton Drive, Dallas, TX 75234
www.unitednotions.com